Crime and the Psychic World

FRED ARCHER

Crime and the Psychic World

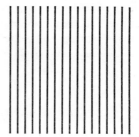

William Morrow and Company, INC.

NEW YORK

To Valerie

who likes a corpse in every chapter

□

The Case of the White Raven

CRIME has always been with us. The first willful action in human history (Biblical version) was to break the law of the Garden of Eden. In the second *de*-generation mankind invented murder. From there on the Old Testament is as much a catalogue of crime as is the *Newgate Calendar.* Or the *News of the World!*

Indeed, Lord Riddell, when chairman of the newspaper which, specializing in reports of the sordid, seamy and salacious aspects of life and conduct, built the largest circulation in the world, answered his critics by saying, "The *News of the World,* like the Bible, records crimes and punishments."

Psychic methods of murder investigation were introduced when Cain slew Abel. ". . . the voice of thy brother's blood crieth unto me from the ground" *(Gen.* 4:10). The god whose name might not be spoken was the first psychic detective. As Solomon, Biblically speaking, was the first psychological detective; and Isaac the first criminal to plant false clues.

Modern psychic detectives may be mediums with Spiritualist convictions; persons with extrasensory powers but no special beliefs; or laymen subject to one or more isolated experiences they might never seek to analyze.

By methods collectively best described as supernormal (*not* supernatural) they may solve crimes; foresee and sometimes prevent crime; even on occasion reveal crimes which no one save the perpetrators knew had been committed.

Many of the people involved in these stories I have known personally, and some of those who vouch for the facts are eminent in their fields. In a number of the more famous cases dealt with here, the psychic contribution towards the solution has not been disclosed, or else has been glossed over lightly, in most previous accounts.

Of course, standards of evidence vary. If it were not so, most scientific disputes need never arise, juries would never disagree, readers would all be of the same opinion . . . and life would be dull indeed! Scientific proof and legal proof are not the same. The repetitive controlled tests which have become the *sine qua non* of modern science are not feasible in most branches of psychical research, owing to the nature of the phenomena. The same applies in some orthodox branches of science! Much of the evidence quoted here would be accepted by a court of law—and has been in some cases.

While this book is concerned with psychic evidence within the context of crime, readers may be interested in the apparent bearing some of it has on the hypotheses of human survival and spirit communication. William James, the Harvard psychologist, who was also in the forefront of psychical research, liked to point out that in order to disprove a belief that all crows are black it would be sufficient to produce one white raven. As I said, standards vary—even standards of whiteness if we believe the soap powder advertisers. So that in a sense, like the elusive bluebird, the white raven bringing proof of survival has to be discovered by each individual for himself.

I have no dogmatic zeal to overturn convictions that crows are black, and it is far from being the purpose of this book to do so. If the reader finds a number of puzzling gray birds . . . well, he can suspect, if he wishes, a white raven lurking somewhere around.

Tracking him down is the most fascinating detective quest of any.

Fred Archer

CONTENTS

☐

INTRODUCTION: *The Case of the White Raven* 5

ONE: *Human Bloodhound Tracked Jack the Ripper* 11

TWO: *No Hiding Place for the Body* 24

THREE: *Mind Readers (and Mounties) Get Their Man* 36

FOUR: *The Stuff of Dreams Is . . . Murder!* 47

FIVE: *Dead Men Do Tell Tales* 61

SIX: *There's a Good Crime Coming* 77

SEVEN: *Murderers from Hell* 90

EIGHT: *A Witch in Time Stops Crime* 107

8   *Crime and the Psychic World*

NINE: *Bury Him Not on the Lone Prairie*   123

TEN: *The Law and the Prophets*   137

ELEVEN: *Not "Private Eyes" but "Psychic Eyes"*   145

TWELVE: *Clairvoyant Crimebusters of Europe*   156

THIRTEEN: *From the Murderer's Viewpoint*   166

FOURTEEN: *The Psychic Eye of Justice*   179

Index   185

For murder, though it have no tongue, will speak
With most miraculous organ

SHAKESPEARE

☐

CHAPTER ONE

Human Bloodhound Tracked Jack the Ripper

SAY "Murder most foul!" and the instant response is "Jack the Ripper!"

A phrase-association test taken by any English man, woman or child for half a century and more would have almost inevitably produced that result. From a high percentage of other Europeans, and Americans, one would have got the same answer. Never before or since has a series of murders excited so much international attention *while still in commission and after*. Without exaggeration, the Jack the Ripper case can be tagged the crime mystery of a century.

This is a bold claim. So let us consider what makes it valid.

The essentials of the Ripper murders can be stated very briefly: with challenging abandon Jack the Ripper butchered his victims in the open streets (with one exception), carved up their bodies in surgical fashion and, with an entire metropolis awaiting his next strike and on the lookout (after the first two killings), always made good his getaway. In that sentence lie the clues.

Attempts have been made to favor the Ripper with astronomical totals of victims. Six murders only can definitely be said to have borne his trademarks. Petiot, Landru and quite a few others would consider six to be only a beginning.

The mutilations he performed were repulsive. Yet he was not so nauseatingly degenerate as the vampiric Kuerten, Alonzo Robinson or the necrophilic Christie, to name only three.

Three things combine to make Jack the Ripper more memorable than other murderers:

First: he killed in the open. Not hidden within his own four walls, not in lonely country byways, but in the densely populated streets of London's East End. Always there was help within earshot, police seldom more than a hundred yards away.

Second: the hue and cry, unprecedented in degree when his crimes were anticipated. Mass murderers are often unheard of until they are safely under arrest. For one grisly autumn Jack the Ripper held London in a grip of terror. Thousands of extra police were drafted into Whitechapel, every citizen watched his neighbor, even the criminal underworld was alerted against him. The head of the Pinkerton agency offered help. The chief of the New York police was consulted—and when he recalled somewhat similar style killings in the States, numbers of Americans became included among the dozens of suspects arrested each day. In Germany, France, Italy and at the ports of other nations, men were held for questioning.

No doubt the sporting element in all this—one man pitting himself against a nation, the world almost—if not consciously appreciated at the time, has been part of the fascination for later generations. Even to the extent of driving Sir Charles Warren, the Commissioner of Police, out of office, Jack the Ripper was the victor.

But the third and most important reason is: he was never caught.

There has never been an official solution. The real mystery remains: who was Jack the Ripper? And why did he stop? To these questions I intend to give an answer.

Of course, plenty of suspects, apart from those arrested, were paraded at the time and have been since. One was a Cabinet Minister. General Booth, founder of the Salvation Army, had doubts about his secretary. Walter Sickert, the painter, held a theory about a veterinary student who had shared his lodgings. Warders of the Tombs, in New York, believed Ameer Ben Ali, a bearded Algerian who came under their care in 1891 after killing and mutilating a waterfront prostitute, to have been Jack the Ripper.

And, not unexpectedly, there were voluntary claimants to the

Ripper's title. Two of them were, indeed, genuine murderers. Neill Cream, the poisoner, confessed on the gallows, "I am Jack!" Frederick Bailey Deeming, who killed his two wives and four children, made the same admission while awaiting execution. Unfortunately for these attempts at greater notoriety both were in jails abroad in 1888 while the Ripper was operating.

Many theories concerning the Ripper's identity have been put forward by writers and criminologists. As recently as 1965 two books were added to the huge pile, one author maintaining that the arch-criminal was an unsuccessful barrister, the other that he was a kosher slaughterer.

I have good reason for suggesting that these theories are wrong. And a logical explanation of why the Ripper murders stopped. They stopped because the murderer was apprehended.

One of the lighter moments in the Jack the Ripper saga was when Sir Charles Warren, the Commissioner of Police, had bloodhounds brought in to track him down. This was a nonsensical idea in the first place. It quickly developed into farce when the bloodhounds, taken to Tooting for a practice run, promptly got lost. Police stations were alerted to look for them.

Nevertheless, the probability is that a bloodhound ultimately did find Jack the Ripper—a human bloodhound. Not by sense of smell, needless to say, but by means of a "sixth sense"—to borrow Charles Richet's term embracing different forms of mental mediumship.

The bloodhound was Robert James Lees, the medium who—as I related in *Exploring the Psychic World**—gave séances to Queen Victoria.

Lees was not a professional medium. He was a man of private means, a scholar and a philanthropist. He helped Gladstone to write a scriptural tract. On his arm the ailing Disraeli took his last walk in London. Looking at it in one way Lees was very nearly the last man in England one could imagine taking part in the hunt for a violent murderer. From another view he was the most likely person to have caught him.

This is how it happened:

One day, in the autumn of 1888, soon after the start of the

* William Morrow & Company, Inc., New York, 1967.

Ripper terror, R. J. Lees, quietly working in his study, was seized by a clairvoyant vision. He saw a man and a woman walking down a mean street, illumined by the glare of light from a gin palace. The hands of the barroom clock, seen through the window, pointed at 12:40.

The woman was obviously half drunk. The man appeared to be sober. He was wearing a suit of dark tweed, and carried a light overcoat. His eyes seemed to glitter in the lamplight.

The couple turned into a narrow court, seeking out a dark corner. Standing against a wall the woman leaned back, invitingly.

The man stepped closer, but not with amorous intent. After a quick glance around to be certain they were alone, he clapped a hand over the woman's mouth. Her feeble, intoxicated struggling had hardly begun before he had cut her throat with a knife. Blood spurted over the man's shirtfront, but he kept his hand to her mouth till he had lowered her to the ground.

Then, with seemingly expert skill, he used the knife to mutilate her body. When he had finished he wiped the blade on the woman's clothes before stowing it away. Finally, he put on the coat he had previously laid aside, buttoning it to hide his bloodied shirt, and unhurriedly walked away.

There the vision ended.

Lees was overwhelmed with horror for he knew he had witnessed a murder not yet committed. When he had sufficiently recovered from the shock he hurried to Scotland Yard.

He was dismayed by his reception. Not surprisingly perhaps, the police treated him as just another of the many cranks who came pestering them with "information" about the Whitechapel killer.

To humor his persistence, the duty sergeant made a note of the time Lees believed that the murder would take place and his description of the scene.

It happened the very next night.

Robert James Lees visited the place of the crime, the scene of his vision, with his manservant. It proved to be more than his sensitive constitution could stand.

"I felt almost as if I was an accessory before the fact," was how he described it. "It made such an impression on me that my whole nervous system was seriously shaken. I could not sleep at night, and under the advice of a physician I removed with my family to the Continent."

Lees was no hardbitten detective. He was a gentle mystic, a religious writer whose interpretations of disputed passages in the Bible drew favorable comment from Archbishops Temple and Benson, Cardinals Newman, Manning and Gibbons.

It is scarcely to be wondered that such an experience should leave him prostrate. More mystifying is why Scotland Yard, the warning having proved true, did not then seek his assistance.

During a short stay abroad Lees was not troubled by further visions.

Soon after his return to London he took his wife on an outing. Heading back home they caught an omnibus at Shepherd's Bush. When it reached Notting Hill a man clambered aboard, a man of medium height wearing a dark tweed suit and a light overcoat.

Once again Lees had the singular sensation that told him he was in "contact" with a murderer.

He whispered urgently to his wife, "That man is Jack the Ripper."

She laughed and told him not to be foolish, but Lees knew he was not mistaken. When the man got off the bus at Marble Arch, Lees left his wife to journey on home and followed him.

The man turned into Park Lane with Lees in pursuit. Halfway down this famous thoroughfare the medium, to his relief, sighted a policeman. Accosting the officer he pointed to the man some distance ahead, and said he knew him to be Jack the Ripper. He demanded that the man be taken into custody.

Like his colleagues at Scotland Yard the constable thought he was dealing with a lunatic. He laughed at Lees, and threatened to run him in when he persisted with his allegations. While the argument was taking place the man in the dark suit had hailed a cab and been driven out of sight.

That night Lees had another psychic preview of murder.

The scene was not so distinct as before, but the victim's face stood out clearly.

She had been mutilated in a peculiar fashion: one ear was completely severed, the other remained hanging by a thin shred of flesh.

Twice-bitten, Lees this time insisted on an interview with a chief inspector when he arrived at Scotland Yard. It made little difference at first. The official treated his story with much the same skepticism his subordinates had shown. Until Lees mentioned the oddity of the ears.

Then his attitude changed. The police had just received a letter via the Central News Agency signed by someone claiming to be Jack the Ripper. The writer promised, as a proof of authenticity, that next time out he would "clip the lady's ears off" and send them to the police.

By dusk the next night more than four thousand police, some disguised as seamen and dock laborers, were patrolling the streets of Whitechapel.

But the Ripper's amazing luck did not desert him. Before dawn he had added two more to his list of atrocities and escaped. He had been interrupted before he could complete his mutilations on the first victim, but a start had been made on severing the ears.

Lees suffered another nervous collapse at the news.

After his recovery he went to dinner one evening at the Criterion Restaurant with two American friends, Roland B. Shaw of New York, and Fred C. Beckwith from Wisconsin.

The three men had started their meal when Lees suddenly exclaimed, "Jack the Ripper has committed another murder!"

For the third time he hastened to Scotland Yard. When the report of this murder came in the police at last considered it worthwhile asking Lees to use his uncanny gifts to help them.

Could he become a human bloodhound and track the murderer to his lair? The medium said he would try. They took him to the scene of the killing, and he made strenuous efforts to get a guiding "scent." With detectives following him he led the way through the streets of London from East End to West End.

Finally, Lees came to a halt in front of an impressive mansion. His face worn and pallid, his eyes bloodshot, he could only gasp in a hoarse whisper, "Inside there is the murderer—the man you are looking for!"

"It's not possible." The chief inspector was crestfallen. The house they were facing was the home of a fashionable and highly reputable physician.

Yet, torn as the officer was by fear of a blunder, the medium's certainty had impressed him. He decided he would push on with the inquiry if Lees could tell him what lay behind the closed door of the house. If his description was seen to be accurate when the door was opened the investigation would be thorough.

Without hesitation Lees said there was a porter's chair of black oak in the hallway to the right, a window of stained glass at one end, and a dog—a large mastiff—sleeping at the foot of the stairs.

They knocked. The door was opened to them by a maid. They saw the oak chair and the stained-glass window, but no mastiff. They questioned the maid. Surprised, she told them that the dog had been sleeping at the bottom of the staircase. She had just let it out into the back garden.

Then the chief inspector began to feel sure of his ground. He asked to speak to the doctor's wife.

Under their questioning it was not long before the woman had made some amazing disclosures. Soon after the start of her marriage, she said, she had discovered that her husband had sudden manias for inflicting pain. Her first awareness of it came one night when, after having gone to bed, she went downstairs again unexpectedly and found him torturing a cat. Too frightened to interfere she returned to her bed before he noticed her presence. Next morning the doctor was his normal, kindly self.

Other incidents followed, each one increasing her suspicion that her husband must be insane. One time he punished his small son for imitating him in an act of cruelty. While he was beating the child a sadistic urge seemed to take control of him, and the servants had to help her restrain him from doing serious harm.

Then recently she had noticed that the nights when her husband was away from home coincided with the East End murders . . . and a great dread had struck her.

When the doctor himself came down and was questioned he admitted that there were intervals when he seemed to have suffered loss of memory. Faced with their suspicion that, perhaps during the lapses to which he confessed, he might have committed the Ripper savageries he was horrified.

In a voluntary statement he said that on a number of occasions he had found himself sitting in his room with the sensation of having wakened after a long stupor. Once he had discovered blood on his shirt. Another time there were scratches on his face.

With the discovery of the notorious tweed suit and light over-coat in an examination of his wardrobe the doctor himself became convinced of his guilt. He begged them to kill him, saying he could not live with the knowledge that he was a monster.

Jack the Ripper did not die.

A specially formed commission on lunacy found him to be insane, and he was sent to an asylum.

Why the hearing was held in private, and the Ripper's identity kept secret has never been satisfactorily explained. It has been claimed that he had highly-placed connections, which is not too unlikely. It has even been suggested that in his professional capacity he had attended one or more members of the royal family, but there is no evidence for this so far as I know.

Whatever the answer, powerful reasons must have been brought to bear to insure silence. Lees was sworn to secrecy, a pledge he never broke, concerning the true identity of Jack the Ripper.

That is the story.

I never knew Robert James Lees, but I was acquainted with his son, Mr. Claude Lees, and have known his daughter, Miss Eva Lees, for many years. His family have always been reluctant to talk about the more sensational aspects of their father's career. Miss Lees is devoted to furthering his main work of propagating a spiritual philosophy. Due to her efforts his six books are always in print.

It was R. J. Lees himself who left a record of his own part in the Jack the Ripper story in a document to be opened after his death. My story is based on his account.

I am well aware that it reads like melodrama. Everything connected with Jack the Ripper is melodrama indeed. More to the point, while it accords for the most part with the generally accepted facts of the Ripper case, there are discrepancies. For example: 12:40 A.M. The first few crimes occurred later than this. Confusion and contradiction are a besetting feature of contemporary reports, but it does appear to be established that these victims were alive till at least 2 A.M. So either the barroom clock was wrong or Lees misread the time. Similarly, he and his American friends must have been having a late dinner indeed if they were still at table when the Ripper killed his last victim. More likely it was a late supper or an early breakfast they were sharing.

However, it would be unwise to dismiss the validity of the main story owing to errors of detail of this kind. They are the sort of mistakes to which a man depending on memory years after the events would be susceptible. R. J. Lees was eighty-one when he died, and forty-three years had then elapsed since the Ripper murders. A journalist or a criminologist would have checked; a theorist trying to make out a case would have correlated his story with the records. Age and time apart, Lees was a man more interested in the inner truth than external appearances.

Like other writers and criminologists one of the first things I did when I went to live in London was to search for the scenes of the Jack the Ripper murders. Some of the street names were changed—another tribute to the Ripper!—and the whole locality has vastly altered, slum clearance being the only benefit derived from Hitler's bombing. But on a foggy November night, even twenty years ago, it was not impossible to imagine what it must have been like in the nineteenth century. And, unless demolished in the last year or two, houses from which the tenants could have watched the Ripper at work are still standing.

I am acquainted with nearly all the published theories, and the R. J. Lees story is to me the most persuasive. Proof is lacking because, for reasons which to him seemed honorable, Lees did not fully reveal the identity of the murderer. Yet, unlike any other theory I know of, the claim here does rest on the word of a named principal actor, who states that he himself was instrumental in bringing the Ripper to book. Lees was no publicity hound, his whole life indicates that association with anything unsavory was abhorrent to him. To the day of his death he held an unblemished reputation, and his word would have been taken without hesitation by everyone who knew him.

Any theory of Jack the Ripper, to be plausible, must account for the surgical skill demonstrated by the murderer, the scope of his operations being confined to the East End, his ability to lull the suspicions of his victims, and the stopping of his crimes so abruptly.

The surgical skill? Well, I find the evidence for Jack the Ripper being medically qualified impressive.

The *Times* stated: "The murderer gives proof of anatomical

skill. Not one man in a thousand could have played the part. . . ." The *Lancet* said: "Obviously the work was that of an expert. . . ."

Dr. Fred Gordon Brown, who examined the body of the fifth victim, Catherine Eddowes, said it was evident from the methodical character of the mutilations that the criminal possessed some anatomical knowledge.

But as not infrequently happens there was a difference of medical opinion. Although the left kidney and another organ had been extracted, Drs. Sequeira and Saunders considered no great anatomical skill had been shown, and that the mutilations did not disclose any design on a particular organ.

The most unambiguous claim that the Ripper must necessarily be a doctor was put forward by the coroner, Mr. Wynne Baxter. At the inquest on Annie Chapman, the third victim, he said:

". . . the injuries have been made by someone who had considerable anatomical skill and knowledge. There are no meaningless cuts. The organ has been taken out by one who knew where to find it, and the difficulties he would have to contend against, and how he would have to use his knife so as to abstract the organ without injury to it. No unskilled person would have known where to find it, or would have recognized it when it was found. For instance, no mere slaughterer of animals could have carried out these operations. It must have been someone accustomed to the postmortem room. . . ."

The divisional surgeon, Dr. Phillips, testified: "I think the anatomical knowledge was only less displayed or indicated by the man being hindered in consequence of haste."

It seems sensible to conclude that the truth rests closer to those who granted a considerable degree of operating skill to Jack the Ripper, rather than to others who denied it him. Doctors guarded the reputations of their colleagues more jealously than the customs of other professions have ever allowed. Putting it mildly, the medical examiners would have a built-in reluctance to agree that a sadistic murderer should be sought exclusively within their ranks so long as the proof could be regarded as less than absolute. Dr. Phillips' evidence is significant, and inclines one to think that some of his colleagues may have overlooked that aspect of the matter to which he draws attention. In addition to the brief time at his disposal, the murderer was hampered by dim and indirect lighting, and had constantly to be looking over his shoulder expecting to find a policeman there. Making their examinations in the same light, possibly supplemented by policemen's lanterns, doctors in two cases failed to notice the nature of the victim's wounds. And they were not distracted by fear of arrest. Working under the Ripper's handicaps, one may wonder how neatly and expeditiously the president of the Royal College of Surgeons could be expected to perform.

Why were the murders confined to the East End? Perhaps the answer is simply because it was far removed geographically, and socially much further, from the West End. A dog does not foul his own doorstep. True enough, prostitutes were to be found for the sacrifice all over London, but their slayer might reasonably prefer the hue and cry to be concentrated away from his home. Had the Ripper lived in Whitechapel, where people were packed in slum houses like human sardines, all privacy at a minimum, it seems highly improbable that his comings and goings could have escaped remark. Equally, of course, in those mean streets an overdressed toff would have stood out like a peacock in a chicken run. Hundreds of people must have seen Jack without suspecting that he was the Ripper. So perhaps we need to look for someone like Chesterton's invisible man, so familiar that though seen he was not noticed. Wherever he came from he must have known the area. If we ask ourselves which group from the upper classes, priests excepted, work and gain acceptance in slum districts everywhere, the answer we come up with is doctors. In fact, medical students at the East End hospitals did come under suspicion. Senior physicians were held more sacrosanct, but at least two doctors were on the short list of police suspects before the end.

What type of man could most easily lull the suspicions of his prospective victims? The distinguished alienist Dr. Forbes Winslow believed that the Ripper must be "of the upper class of society." The descriptions given by several witnesses who *may* have seen the murderer accord with this view. Certainly no obvious ruffian would fit the role at a time when every woman walking the streets half expected she would be the next victim; when the panic had reached such proportions that one suggestion was that prostitutes should be equipped with whistles and revolvers or, funnier still, accompanied on their rounds by vigilantes. The stranger who could persuade these women to go off with him to find a dark corner was surely a man whose physical aspect aroused no qualms, and a persuasive talker. Maybe "Dr. Jack" practiced his bedside manner.

All this gives the outline of a man who, in social and professional standing, near enough matches the murderer portrayed by R. J. Lees. Is there supporting evidence that the Ripper stopped because he was caught and ended up in an asylum? Scotland Yard has kept official silence on the subject. Edwin T. Woodhall, a former detective-sergeant and later a member of the British secret service, declares that the Lees story was more than once told to him by older hands during his years at the Yard, and I have heard the same from other sources.

And there is a startlingly coincidental story told by Dr. Harold Dearden, the well-known writer and criminologist.

One day in November, 1918, Dr. Dearden and a companion were celebrating the latter's fortieth birthday in surroundings somewhat less than harmonious—a dugout on the Somme. These circumstances led Dearden's friend to remark that his tenth birthday also had been ruined—by Jack the Ripper.

His story was that his father, a widower, then ran a private mental asylum situated on the outskirts of London. As a birthday treat he had promised his son a visit to the theater. At the last moment the outing was canceled, due to the arrival of an unexpected new patient. The boy caught a glimpse of the patient surrounded by attendants, and later he came to know him. But before he was old enough to ask questions his father had died and he was living abroad with an uncle.

Three things he did know.

The patient was the son of one of his father's oldest friends. It is a fair assumption that the majority of the father's old friends belonged to his own class, that many would be medical colleagues whose sons were likely (more so in Victorian England than today) to have followed them in the same profession.

The patient was ambidextrous. So was Jack the Ripper, in the opinion of experts who saw his handiwork.

The boy's tenth birthday fell on November 9, 1888. Jack the Ripper had given his uniquely dramatic farewell performance the night before. And, publicly, was never to be heard from again.

☐

CHAPTER TWO

No Hiding Place for the Body

THE very idea that Jack the Ripper could have been tracked down by psychic means must appear incredible to many. So it would be if it stood as a solitary instance. As it happens, however, plenty of criminal cases have been solved by similar methods. And while in the Ripper case much is hidden in the mists of time, in some modern cases the facts can be fully established.

When Mae West came to London to appear in *Diamond Lil* I attended several séances with her, at the Savoy Hotel where she was staying and at a medium's home in North London. In contrast with her public image, the "Come up and see me some-time" star is in private life a sensitive, religious-minded woman. During this period some jewelry belonging to Miss West was stolen from her dressing room at the Prince of Wales Theatre where her show was running. After police inquiries had made little progress, Mae West put in a transatlantic call to a medium friend, Jack Kelly, to ask if he could trace the thief.

Mae West chose Kelly because she had already had several examples of his ability as a psychic detective. On one occasion Los Angeles police, seeking a murder suspect, called on her in Hollywood, and to help them she phoned Jack Kelly, who was 2,000 miles away in Buffalo. Before Mae West could finish telling him what was wanted, Kelly interrupted her, saying, "The man was arrested twenty minutes ago." It took the detectives ten minutes to pull themselves together and contact police headquarters in Los Angeles. News had just come through, they learned, that the wanted man had been picked up in San Diego within the last half hour.

On the problem of the missing jewels Jack Kelly at once described a man he said was an employee of the theater, and gave the initial of his name. The identification was sufficiently clear that by pursuing the matter through police channels evidence could probably have been obtained for a prosecution. But as I have indicated, Mae West is a magnanimous person. She decided that she did not wish the thief to be punished.

Mae West is a Spiritualist, and Spiritualists and their guides, as distinct from those clairvoyants who claim no special religious affiliation, are very often reluctant to be used in tracking criminals. This is partly an unwillingness to have dealings with unsympathetic officials—after all, up to 1951 mediums in England were legally classed as "rogues and vagabonds," and subject to prosecution under laws which did not permit evidence that genuine phenomena had been produced to be put forward as a defense. But mainly, in murder cases, it is because their beliefs are opposed to capital punishment.

However, there are crimes so vile that on occasion these considerations may be overruled. Such a case began with the disappearance of Mona Tinsley.

Mona, a ten-year-old child, ran joyously from school on the afternoon of January 5, 1937—and never reached home. A search was started locally near Newark-on-Trent where she lived. Soon it had spread far afield. Bloodhounds were utilized at an early stage. Boy Scouts, hiking clubs, divers and even water diviners were enrolled as the hunt swept across open country with rivers and canals.

Finally a friend of the Tinsley family sought the aid of Estelle Roberts. I have known Estelle Roberts for more than twenty years, and consider her the most versatile of present-day mediums. Famous on the public platform, she has given séances to royalty and has demonstrated clairvoyance to members of Parliament within the chambers of that law-making institution itself —breaking the law with their encouragement in so doing.

When Estelle Roberts agreed to try and help in the Tinsley case, Mona's parents persuaded the Newark police to send her a pink silk dress the child had worn. This was to establish a point of contact. Soon after she began to handle it the medium felt herself to be in communication with Mona.

The little girl was dead. Strangled. Estelle Roberts was made aware of the house to which Mona had been taken by her abductor: there was a ditch at one side, full of water, a field at the back, and nearby, a graveyard. In the distance a public house could be seen. Then, clairvoyantly, Estelle saw herself being taken by the dead girl through the graveyard, over a bridge and across fields to a river.

She telephoned the Newark police. When she told them about the house and its surroundings they did not conceal their surprise. She had described the home of Frederick Nodder, a 45-year-old laborer they had just detained on suspicion of having abducted the missing girl. Mona's body had still not been found, and evidence was lacking to justify a charge of murder.

The police were so impressed that they invited Estelle Roberts to visit the scene of the crime—unofficially. They could not openly invite her to go to Newark and break the law. What they actually said was that if she arrived at Newark station she would find a car waiting to pick her up.

Estelle accepted the semi-invitation, and took the next available train from her home in Esher, Surrey.

As promised, a police car met her at Newark. She was driven to the village of Newington, thirty-five miles outside the city. She stepped out of the car and saw before her a house she recognized from her vision.

As one familiar with the place she went in in front of the detectives, entering through a side door and making straight for an upstairs back bedroom. In this room, she told them when they followed, Mona had been murdered.

The police already had evidence that the child had been held prisoner there.

Estelle said that Mona had spent some of her time copying out of a book. Pieces of paper she had scribbled on had been found and identified.

Yet without a body there was no proof, though the medium insisted it had happened so, that Mona Tinsley had been strangled.

Indeed, Estelle Roberts went further: the murderer, she said, had then put the body in a sack and carried it out through the side door.

Why the side door she could not say. The police knew that Nodder had kept his front door permanently closed.

They asked if she knew where Nodder had hidden the body. She said she would try to show them.

Estelle Roberts led the way out of the house, through the garden, into the graveyard, over the bridge spanning a canal, and across several fields . . . all these the landmarks she had seen clairvoyantly.

She stopped when they came to the banks of the River Idle. There she pointed to a stretch of water and flatly stated, "The body lies in there."

Whatever faith the police had begun to have in her vanished at that point, and their normal skepticism reasserted itself. The river had been dragged, thoroughly. They were certain there was no body.

Estelle Roberts is the most confident of mediums, and probably the one with most reason for confidence. She went back home never doubting she was right, but unable to shake the resistance of the detectives. Their search was extended to cover three counties.

Not until every other effort had proved abortive was the advice of the rejected medium acted upon. Then the section of river she had indicated was dragged again and the body of Mona Tinsley discovered.

Afterwards, Chief Constable Barnes, who had been in charge of the investigation, made amends with this bluntly spoken tribute:

"Short of jumping in the damned river and fishing the body out herself, she took us to it."

At the trial of Frederick Nodder it emerged that the crime took place exactly as Estelle Roberts had reconstructed it. Mona Tinsley was *strangled* in the *back bedroom,* her body put *in a sack,* and carried out through the *side door.*

Nodder was found guilty of murder and hanged on New Year's Day, 1938.

Unwillingness on the part of the police to accept mediumistic aid is understandable, particularly when they do not know with whom they are dealing. Bear in mind that whenever a sensational crime hits the headlines, officers conducting the case are swamped with crank messages, farfetched theories and crazy confessions.

Superintendent Percy Ellington, chief of the Nottingham C.I.D., is one of the—fortunately not too rare—officials who do not dismiss the idea that such help can be of value. And he found that it paid off.

After he had brought to trial the killer of Mrs. Jane Legg the Superintendent said: "It is a most unusual circumstance for information of this sort really to help us, but there is no doubt that in this instance it did help us to pinpoint the murderer."

Mrs. Jane Legg, an old lady of eighty-eight, was found dead at her home on November 2, 1951. Next day her daughter-in-law, Mrs. Flora Blower, sent her son Derek to consult Mrs. Ann Jones, a medium at the Carrington Road Spiritualist Church.

Mrs. Jones told Derek that a man aged between thirty and forty was closely involved in the death of Mrs. Legg. The man was a relative of the old lady and, she added, his hair was changing color.

At that stage murder had not been established. The Blowers did not know the manner in which death had come to Mrs. Legg. When they learned that the police had decided it was murder, the husband, Mr. William Blower, called on Superintendent Ellington. He told him what the medium had said.

The result of this interview was to put the police on the trail of Blower's nephew, Albert Bradley Radford. He fitted the medium's description having, as Blower could tell them, a distinctive patch of white hair.

Twenty-four hours later Radford was found in Manchester and detained. C.I.D. men brought him back to Nottingham.

At a séance with Mrs. Jones following Radford's arrest, a number of facts were given to Mrs. Blower which, if already known to the police, had not been made public.

The medium said that Radford had first argued with his grandmother, then had knocked her down and struck her with a weapon that "opened and shut." He afterwards got rid of the weapon by throwing it into water. Some other object he had flung into the coal fire blazing in the hearth.

The evidence presented at the court hearing indicated that Radford had stabbed Mrs. Legg with a penknife, which he later dropped down a drain. He had robbed her of her purse and taken out the money, then thrown the purse on the fire.

The jury's verdict on Albert Bradley Radford, killer of his own grandmother, was guilty but insane.

Saddest part of a tragic story is that a catastrophe of some kind had been foreseen by Mrs. Jones months before it happened. Early that year she had warned Mr. and Mrs. Blower to "watch out for trouble in November." Of course, this was much too vague a prophecy for murder to be prevented by it.

Prevision of crimes and the vexing question of psychic intervention will be discussed in later chapters. For the moment, to counteract any impression that extrasensory perception will always succeed when police procedure has failed, I want to refer to a case that stumped everybody.

My old editor, Stuart Martin, a man with years of experience in England and America as a crime reporter, was the first to tell me some of the remarkable feats of Gene Dennis.

A Kansas girl, Eugenie Dennis came into prominence while still a teen-ager through her clairvoyant gift. She helped the police of several western states to clear up minor cases. In Joplin, Missouri, she traced fifteen stolen bicycles. At Chillicothe she gave officers the name of the street and number of the house where they could catch up with a parole breaker—in St. Louis. In Omaha she was instrumental in recovering twenty-three vanished diamonds. She was tested by the police department of New York, Chief Commissioner Enright, Commissioners Faurot and Shaw, and Inspector Fay taking part in the experiment.

At the time of the Brighton Trunk Crime No. 1, as the sensational case was to become known, Gene Dennis was on a visit to England.

The horrifying discovery of a trunk containing a woman's torso was made by a luggage clerk at Brighton railway station on June 17. From the number of the ticket, G 1945, officials were able to deduce that the trunk had been deposited at the cloakroom on June 6—Derby Day—during the busiest hours.

Soon after reading the first accounts in the London newspapers, Gene Dennis telephoned Chief Constable Hillier of Brighton. Her name was unknown to him then, and he dismissed her offer of assistance. Miss Dennis was not daunted by this. She went down to Brighton and, avoiding the Chief Constable, obtained an interview with the superintendent in charge of the investigation. She managed to persuade him to allow her to handle the piece of cord—six yards of the type used in venetian blinds—which had been tied around the brown paper covering the torso.

Her estimates of the age and height of the victim, and a statement that the woman had been pregnant, were confirmed when Sir Bernard Spilsbury announced the result of his postmortem. Spilsbury, eminent pathologist and perfect witness, stood next to God in the English law courts—some judges and juries would even have doubted the Almighty had Spilsbury disagreed.

Gene Dennis made a prediction that owing to this crime another murder would be uncovered. In the weeks that followed, a quick solution to the crime not being forthcoming, the police subjected large sections of Brighton to a house-to-house search. At 52 Kemp Street, a locked and empty lodging house, a second trunk containing a corpse was discovered.

Yet the clairvoyant missed the mark in saying that the origin of the brown paper wrapped around the first torso would be traced, and that would lead them to the murderer. It seemed a promising clue, and the investigators concentrated on it for weeks and months, but with no success.

Indeed, the Brighton Trunk Crime No. 1 is notable for the amount of effort put into the investigation and the contrastingly meager results. Checks instituted at every railway station in Britain produced from King's Cross terminal a pair of legs which matched up with the torso. What became of the head and the arms is still a mystery.

The police traced 732 girls on the missing persons list. Private doctors and hospitals were canvassed for women who had sought prenatal care in recent months. One London hospital alone had dealt with 5,000 patients during the relevant period, and the detectives accounted for all save fifteen.

Despite such great activity neither the police nor mediums ever managed to identify the victim. Still less did they succeed in bringing the killer to account. In fact, although the circumstances make it appear probable, there is no certainty that a murder took place.

Sir Bernard Spilsbury would go no further than to say that death was probably due to a blow on the head. The coroner could record nothing more positive than the unsatisfactory verdict: "Found dead."

Murderers often attempt to get rid of the body in the belief that without the corpse on display they cannot be brought to trial. This is not the law, a lesson some have had a limited, though undisturbed, period to reflect upon in the death cell. Sometimes an accused person has lost whatever chance he had of proving his innocence by having too-successfully disposed of the remains. James Camb, who pushed the dead body of Gay Gibson through a porthole of the liner *Durban Castle,* put forward the defense that she died of natural causes as a sequel to sexual intercourse. Medically speaking, this was not implausible. Unfortunately, the only evidence which might have supported his plea he had thrown to the fishes. Like Robinson, the Charing Cross Trunk Murderer (more of whom in another chapter), Camb found out that juries, occasionally sympathetic to a nice clean murder, are invariably sensitive about outrage to a corpse. And from the investigators' point of view, while the body need not be essential for a prosecution, it usually helps to have it around.

Finding missing bodies is a branch of detection in which mediums are particularly adept, it would seem. During the years I was a newspaper editor I came across perhaps a dozen such instances in England, and double the number reported from abroad.

The arrival on my desk of copy from a Durban correspondent brought first news of what was soon to be described as "one of the most fiendish crimes in South African criminology."

Myrna Joy Aken, an attractive eighteen-year-old girl, went to catch her homeward-bound bus as usual after finishing work on October 2, 1956. She did not reach home that night, or ever again.

Her parents reported Joy's disappearance to the police and routine inquiries were started. Early reports were negative, and the search quickly spread to cover the whole of South Africa.

After the family had suffered eight days of mounting distress, Joy's brother Colin suddenly had an idea. The father of his old school friend, Jack Palmer, was a medium. To consult him could do no harm.

Nelson Palmer, London-born, sixty-three years old, the retired headmaster of a Durban school for colored pupils, was known to me as a Spiritualist well respected in South Africa. He was not a professional medium, though he had conducted séances at home with his family for thirty years.

At Colin Aken's request, Jack Palmer invited him home to meet his father. Nelson Palmer agreed to hold an impromptu séance.

Palmer went into trance, and soon he was describing a place he said was about sixty miles from Durban on the south coast road. Joy Aken was dead, murdered, and her body was lying in a culvert near stagnant water in that area.

After the séance the message was discussed. Palmer offered to lead a search party. Colin and Jack, Graham Aken, Joy's other brother, and a friend, Reg Utterson, all were anxious to go with him.

They drove out of Durban along the south coast road. Just over a mile north of a village called Umtwalumi, sixty miles from the city, Palmer felt they had come to the neighborhood he was seeking. When he sighted a sluggish watercourse he knew a long search would not be necessary.

A little while later they discovered the culvert, eight feet below the level of the road. Palmer climbed down to it first. He wanted to ease the shock that was awaiting his young companions.

Peering into the concrete drain he saw, not far inside, a pair of feet. The dead girl had been rammed into the pipe headfirst.

Quietly Palmer suggested that Colin should go for the police.

Hardened detectives were shocked by the mutilations on the naked body of Myrna Joy Aken. How long the corpse, which had already lain there for eight days, would have gone undiscovered had it not been for the medium's uncanny power is impossible to say.

When a man was arrested and brought to trial for the murder of Joy Aken, Nelson Palmer was called upon to give evidence in court. He had to explain the basis of his beliefs as a Spiritualist, and how his psychic ability had made it possible for him to find the body of the missing girl. It was the first time testimony of this nature had been admitted by a South African court.

During the next few weeks, as a result of much front-page publicity, Nelson Palmer was inundated with requests to find missing people, buried treasure, even lost cows. Having no desire to use his gifts in this manner he ignored the appeals, except for a few from people in real distress.

Among these were the relatives of Dr. John Philips, who was believed to have defaulted bail on a charge of abortion.

The police had been seeking Dr. Philips for two weeks, but not unnaturally his family were worried about his disappearance from a somewhat different viewpoint.

Nelson Palmer told them what had become of the doctor, but it was not comforting news he had to offer. "You will find his body near water," he informed Dr. Philips' family, "lying in dense bush about five hundred yards northwest of where he lived."

The area had supposedly been covered by the police dragnet. However, a private search was organized.

A party of four monks and five Zulus came upon the doctor's body, propped against a tree on the bank of a river, roughly five hundred yards from home. By his side was an empty bottle.

Missing body findings, so to speak, crop up regularly in psychic history. One such case convinced William James of the reality of psychic phenomena. The famous Harvard psychologist —and brother of Henry James, who wrote that most subtly terrifying of all ghost stories, *The Turn of the Screw*—became president of the Society for Psychical Research in London and a founder of the American S.P.R.

Several countries have featured in the modern examples I have dealt with, and for a final case we go to France. An American author and journalist, Warrington Dawson, was for many years my Paris correspondent. Among the highlights of a distinguished career he had been private secretary to ex-President Theodore Roosevelt, a secret agent for General Joffre in the first world war, and founder and first director of the Paris bureau of United Press.

One story sent by Warrington Dawson was the sensation of Paris in the spring of 1952.

Madame Binet, a seamstress in Montmartre, was surprised when her assistant, Madame Reine Metivet, failed to come to work on the morning of Friday, March 14. Unable to conceive what misfortune might have befallen her, Mme. Binet was understandably concerned.

The previous night Mme. Binet had walked most of the way home with her assistant, who was also her old and intimate friend. Mme. Metivet, as the result of a severe illness, had been a deaf-mute since childhood. But her general health was good and she was very reliable at her job.

That evening Mme. Binet went round to her friend's apartment. She knocked on the door again and again without getting an answer. Next morning, fearing now that because of her deafness Mme. Metivet might have been involved in a street accident, Mme. Binet went to the police.

No traffic accident in which Mme. Metivet could have been a victim had been reported, they told her after checking their lists.

More concerned than ever, Mme. Binet then called upon her friend Mme. Barbier-Morin who, though not a professional medium, had a good reputation in her own circle as a clairvoyant.

Mme. Barbier-Morin had no acquaintance with the missing woman, and Mme. Binet gave her no information. She just produced a photograph and a worker's card belonging to Mme. Metivet, and said quite simply, "Will you try to see for me where this lady now is and what she is doing?"

For a few moments the clairvoyant concentrated in silence. She then said: "The woman who owns this card is not living. I see her lying crushed under a heap of stones, not far from where we are now. I see a red lantern burning. There is also a stairway, but she did not go down the stairs."

Mme. Binet begged for more explicit details that would enable her to find the place.

"I cannot tell you where the street is exactly," Mme. Barbier-Morin said. "I only know that it is in this neighborhood. I can also tell you that, although her body is horribly mangled, the face has remained uninjured. I see it as clearly as in this photograph."

With this information Mme. Binet had to be content. She hurried back to the police station. Although skeptical of indications proffered by a medium, the officials saw where there might be a connection.

A long, high wall had crumbled suddenly in the Rue du Chevalier-de-Labarre. One Mme. Marcoz had been taking her two little dogs for an airing at the time. She had had a narrow escape with one of the animals. The other dog had been crushed to death. But Mme. Marcoz had been certain there was no one else in the street when the wall fell. Firemen had found what remained of the dog in the rubble, but nothing else.

However, as required by law, a red lantern had been placed at the spot as a danger warning. And it so happened that there was a stairway in the street. On account of these details, which did fit in with the clairvoyant message, the police promised a more intensive search.

The next day, Sunday, the mangled body of Mme. Metivet was dug out from under the masonry, a good distance away from where the dog had been buried.

Strangely, the face of the unfortunate woman had altogether escaped injury. She was, as Mme. Barbier-Morin had said, as clearly recognizable as in her photograph.

In this instance, what might have been a crime proved on investigation to be a purely accidental death.

Yet as a feat of clairvoyant aid in solving a mystery it is impressive. For in this case there was no criminal who knew, no living person who knew, apparently, what had happened to the vanished seamstress.

CHAPTER THREE

☐

Mind Readers (and Mounties)
Get Their Man*

IF the art of murder is to conceal murder then for three years the case of Scotty McLauchlan ranked as the perfect crime.

Scotty, a popular figure in the life of the little town of Beechy, Saskatchewan, had told people he was selling his share of the farm to his partner, John Schumacher, and taking the night train to British Columbia.

Friends were at the railroad depot to see him off, but Scotty never arrived at his destination.

His disappearance caused quite a stir. And, of course, there was gossip. Scotty was alleged to have quarreled with two men over girls. Nothing much emerged to substantiate the rumors, certainly no evidence that a crime had been committed. What had happened to Scotty was a mystery, and seemed likely to remain one.

Scotty McLauchlan vanished on January 16, 1930.

Nearly three years later, on the evening of December 10, 1932, Constable Carey of the Royal Canadian Mounted Police walked into Beechy's motion picture house.

The attraction which brought local farmers into town that night was not a film show. They had come to be entertained by a

* For information on which the two stories of "the Mounties" in this chapter are based I am indebted to articles by Philip H. Godsell, F.R.G.S., which appeared in *Fate* magazine.—F.A.

mind reader, a tall, gray-haired man who called himself Professor Gladstone.

The show began.

In the middle of his act the Professor made a dramatic pause. His eye fixed on rancher Bill Taylor. When he spoke, his words jerked the entire audience to attention.

"You are thinking of your friend Scotty McLauchlan. He was murdered. Brutally murdered."

Before the murmurs of astonishment had died down Gladstone's pointing finger had swung round to Constable Carey.

"That's him! The man in the red coat there. He will find the body—and I shall be with him when he does!"

The hall rocked with excitement. Everyone present knew that Bill Taylor had been a close friend of Scotty McLauchlan, and the rancher's expression showed plainly that the mind reader had indeed read his thoughts.

If Bill Taylor was startled, so was Constable Carey. The next day the Mountie phoned his headquarters at Saskatoon, and spoke to Corporal Jack Woods. After a checkup on the mind reader's reputation, Woods went posthaste to Beechy to reopen the case. The sensation Gladstone had created, the Corporal reasoned, might have put the "sod busters" in the mood for talking if nothing else.

The two Mounties, Woods and Carey, visited the snowbound homesteads one after another. They took Gladstone along with them. Again they listened to the popular rumor that Scotty's disappearance must have been the outcome of a jealous quarrel. An explosion of interest had been triggered off by the mind reader's bombshell and it was now more talked about than ever. Folk were recollecting that one of Scotty's rivals had later married the girl.

Yet before nightfall a somewhat different slant on the case was given them. A farmer, awed by the uncanny knowledge of his affairs displayed by Gladstone, admitted that Schumacher, McLauchlan's partner, had one day called on him in a violent rage, making threats to kill the "damned Scotsman."

With this information the Mounties and the mind reader drove out to Schumacher's farm that same night. They were met by a hired hand, who informed them that the boss had gone off to town.

While they waited Professor Gladstone stood gazing over the snow-blanketed farm.

"Scotty McLauchlan's body is around here somewhere," he said. "I know it."

When John Schumacher, a fair-haired giant of a man, came home he would only repeat the story he had told at the time of Scotty's disappearance. He had bought out his partner for a few hundred dollars, which he paid. He had no idea where Scotty went to when he left.

The Mounties asked questions. Schumacher lapsed into a sullen silence. Then Gladstone intervened.

"I'll tell you what happened. Scotty went over to the barn. You followed him and started a quarrel. There was a fight and Scotty fell. You struck, and struck, and struck . . . then you buried his body near the barn."

Schumacher's face was drained of color. He licked dry lips, but stubbornly refused to talk.

A digging party was organized the next day and proceeded to the barn. Professor Gladstone pointed to a pile of manure.

"Under there you'll find all that remains of Scotty."

The men worked with picks and shovels in the freezing cold. When two hours had gone by the Mounties were ready to give up hope. Then one of the diggers unearthed a woolen sock. They carried on after that and soon careful spadework brought into view a full skeleton. Shreds of rotted clothing hung on the fleshless bones.

"It's Scotty all right!" exclaimed one of the party. "I'd know that scarf and mackinaw anywhere."

An examination of their grisly find revealed triple fractures of the skull. Faced with that evidence John Schumacher broke silence and admitted his guilt.

The Mounties always get their man—but sometimes they need a psychic eye to lead them to him!

More than one police department in Canada had cause to appreciate the strange talent of another thought reader, Dr. Maximilien Langsner, late of Vienna, and onetime pupil of Freud.

The most celebrated case in which Dr. Langsner lent assistance when the police were at a loss was the multiple murder on the Booher ranch near Mannville, Alberta. The Booher case features in a number of crime anthologies but, so far as I am aware, only ex-Chief of Police Mike Gier has given full credit for the solution to Dr. Langsner. Chief Gier was, of course, the man who really knew.

Constable Olson, the first policeman to reach the scene of the crime, was summoned to the Booher ranch on the evening of July 9, 1928. Waiting there to meet him were Henry Booher, the rancher; Vernon Booher, his youngest son; Charles Stevenson, a neighbor; and the medical practitioner, Dr. Heaslip, who had sent for the police.

In the kitchen was the body of Mrs. Booher, who had been shot three times in the back of the neck. In another room lay Fred Booher, her son, killed by a bullet through the mouth. In the nearby bunkhouse a hired hand, Gabriel Cromby, had died of head and chest wounds.

The constable was told that Vernon Booher, out working in the fields, had heard shots from the direction of the ranch house at around eight o'clock. Hurrying home he had first found the body of his mother, then that of his brother. Cromby's death he had discovered when he went to the bunkhouse for help.

A second cowhand worked on the ranch, a man named Rosyk. It seemed possible that Rosyk would know something about the shootings so they undertook a search for him. They found Rosyk in one of the barns . . . with two bullet holes strongly proclaiming his innocence.

Four people dead. No robbery. No known enemies. On the face of it a wholly mysterious and motiveless massacre. Police investigation established that the shooting had been done with a .303 rifle, but got no further.

Seeing no prospect of a quick solution to the case, Chief Gier made up his mind to send for Dr. Langsner, with whose work he was acquainted. He well knew the criticism that awaited him if the mind reader failed.

The doctor arrived in time to be present at the inquest.

Neighbors of the Boohers testified to having heard gunshots between six thirty and eight o'clock the evening of the murders, but in that part of the country the noise of shooting was common enough to not require immediate investigation.

Vernon Booher admitted he must have heard shots previous to those which had drawn him back to the ranch house. Charles Stevenson had told him some time before he intended going after a fox which had been troubling the neighborhood, and this he had assumed explained the firing.

Stevenson, a nervous witness, had the spotlight thrown on him as a possible suspect. He admitted that he owned a .303 rifle. Questioned further, he claimed that it had been stolen.

Could he say when the theft took place? Yes, the rifle must have been taken from his closet the Sunday before the murders while he was at church. He had seen the gun there before he left the house and when he returned, it was missing.

It was common custom locally, the way Stevenson told it, for neighbors to drop in and borrow things without permission. If he had needed a gun at any time he would have thought nothing of taking one from the Boohers' house in their absence.

The surviving Boohers, Henry and Vernon, could neither of them have borrowed Stevenson's gun, it appeared. Both had been present at the church service he attended.

Chief Gier called a conference after the inquest. Dr. Langsner and two officers who had been working on the case, Inspector Longacre and Detective Leslie, were invited.

The only course open to them, the policemen concluded, was to make an intensive search for the rifle. Dr. Langsner remained so silent that he was asked, mainly in jest, whether he could already name the killer.

When, very calmly, he said he could, they thought he in turn might be joking.

To call his bluff, if bluff it was, they demanded the name.

"Vernon Booher."

And Langsner went on to relate how, while in court, he had sensed the turmoil in Booher's mind. More specifically, when Stevenson gave evidence of the rifle being stolen, Booher's thoughts had been concentrated on the weapon and where he had hidden it.

Their interest aroused, the detectives were eager to know the hiding place.

The rifle, Langsner said, was concealed in a patch of prairie grass, behind the Booher house to the west.

They took him out to the Booher ranch to show them the exact location.

For a few moments Langsner wandered around, orienting his vision with the surrounding reality. The policemen watched him hopefully, yet still having doubts. Eventually he chose his direction, and took a straight line past the bunkhouse. Soon he came to a halt, concentrating with eyes closed, a hand to his forehead. He gave a satisfied exclamation.

"Take ten steps forward," Langsner directed Detective Leslie.

The policeman took big strides, counting as he went. At the ninth step he stumbled over something lying hidden in the prairie grass. The others hurried forward as Leslie bent down to look. There was the rifle.

No fingerprints showed on the weapon. Langsner said Vernon had wiped it clean and tests proved he was correct.

Although they were now convinced that Vernon Booher was the murderer, Chief Gier had no evidence to justify charging him with the crime. The most he could do was to take Vernon in as a material witness.

How to get the evidence? Dr. Langsner suggested trying a method that had worked before when he was assisting the police at Vancouver. In a robbery case, with a suspect under arrest, the police could not find the jewels he was believed to have stolen. In order to get the information required, all Langsner asked was half an hour in the company of the suspect, not to question him, not even to talk, but merely to be there, silently attuning to his thoughts. This was allowed, and at the end of the stipulated period Langsner was able to report that the stolen jewels were hidden behind a picture in a room with yellow walls. The thief had a girl friend, yellow was her choice in color schemes, and in her apartment they found the loot.

Chief Gier agreed to a similar experiment. A chair was placed outside Vernon Booher's cell so Langsner could sit and observe him. Vernon stared back at him through the bars, pleasantly talkative at first, then curious, finally angry when Langsner refused to speak to him at all.

By that time Langsner had got what he wanted. The biggest

puzzle all along had been the apparent lack of motive. The murders seemed to have benefited no one. Now Langsner knew that an insane hatred of his mother was the force that unleashed Vernon's outburst of violence. His brother, Fred, had heard the shots, and had been killed when he came to investigate. The two cowhands were shot later on when Vernon, getting scared, had convinced himself they could become witnesses against him.

Dr. Langsner also claimed to have the means of breaking Vernon's alibi for the time when Stevenson's rifle had been stolen. So far no one had come forward to deny that Vernon was in church as he said he was. According to Langsner, Vernon had managed to slip away long enough to take the rifle, hide it and be back in church before the end of the service. And there was a witness. A woman, as Langsner described her, with small eyes, a long jaw and wearing a poke bonnet. She had been sitting near the back of the church, to the left of the door, and had noticed Vernon leave and afterwards return.

Within twenty-four hours the police identified the lady. Erma Higgins, a spinster, testified that she had seen Booher sneak out of church and in again.

Chief Gier arranged a confrontation. Vernon Booher was brought into the room where Miss Higgins sat. Before he could prepare himself she said, "Vernon, I saw you leave church the day Charlie's rifle was stolen."

Booher said, defeatedly, "I know you did." Then he broke down, sobbing, and confessed to the murders.

It was, as Langsner had discovered, his mother whom Vernon had wanted to kill. The pitiful family tragedy had its start when Vernon brought home a girl friend. Mrs. Booher thought her an unsuitable match for her son and had ordered her out of the house. When, repeatedly, his mother spoke scathingly of the girl and poured ridicule on Vernon himself for being so enamored, his hatred grew. At the end it could find fulfillment only in murder. Four people died to assuage his wounded feelings.

Vernon Booher was found guilty and suffered the death penalty.

One of the toughest and most tenacious officers who gave real substance to the legend that the Mounties always get their man was Staff Sergeant Andy Anderson. There was a famous case though, when to begin with opinion was almost unanimous that the stubborn sergeant had got the wrong man.

In the late summer of 1904 two men made camp on the Cree Indian reservation at Sucker Lake. One was a big, bearded Englishman, who wore a shining buckle on his belt and was followed everywhere by a yellow dog. Two young Indians who visited the white men were amused to see him sewing leather over the stock of his gun, pushing the needle through the hide with a glove that had no fingers.

After two days the Englishman disappeared. Surprisingly, his horses and the dog had not gone with him. His partner, Charlie, stayed another three days—and when he left had to drag the Englishman's dog away from the camp.

This was the story Staff Sergeant Anderson heard from Indians who stopped him on the trail to the Lesser Slave Lake settlement where he was heading. He rode back with them to the reservation.

The first thing Anderson noted at the camp site was the amount of ashes. In warm weather, such as it had been, he would not have expected the campers to need more than just a small fire for cooking. Riffling through the debris he found several fragments of bone. Maybe from meat they had eaten, maybe not.

While searching, Anderson had the suspicion he was being watched, and thought he glimpsed a figure merging silently into the forest when he looked up.

He was in an undecided frame of mind when he left the camp. Did the Indians know more than they had told, or did the missing partner hold the solution to the mystery?

On reaching the settlement at Lesser Slave Lake, Anderson dropped in to see Moise Gladu, not quite knowing what had led him there. The first thing he noticed in the cabin was the number of traps lying around.

He passed a comment, and Gladu smiled. The traps, he said, belonged to a man who was waiting to take the steamer to Edmonton. He wanted to sell them. The man's name? Charlie King.

At that moment a stranger entered the cabin, a stranger the sergeant thought he recognized from the description given him by the Indians. The Englishman's partner. It was Charlie King.

With an appearance of frankness King talked about his trip

through the territory. He had joined up with a stranger named Leaman. After they camped together on the reservation, Leaman had set out on foot on a prospecting trip to Sturgeon Lake.

Anderson found the latter part of the story difficult to believe, but it had to be investigated. He sent Constable Lowe to Sturgeon Lake, with orders to check at every Indian camp and with anyone he met on the trail who might have seen the bearded Englishman.

When Lowe returned a week later, having found no trace of the missing man, Staff Sergeant Anderson took the gamble of arresting Charlie King just as he was about to embark on the S.S. *Midnight Sun* for Edmonton. Anderson felt pretty sure that King was guilty of murder, but he knew he needed much more evidence to gain a conviction.

Unknown to the Mountie—and had he known he would hardly have credited it—an "eyewitness" account of the crime he was laboriously piecing together had appeared in a British newspaper before Anderson himself knew the Englishman was missing. A man who could identify the murderer would soon be on board a ship crossing the Atlantic.

Meanwhile the sergeant pressed on with the search for material clues.

From a slough near the camp site he dredged up a number of objects, notably a silver buckle, a nugget tiepin and a sovereign case. The buckle was recognized by an Indian as the one on the Englishman's belt.

The investigation switched to Edmonton. A saddler there had sold a sewing-palm (the glove without fingers which the Indian boys found amusing) to a man headed for Peace River.

A Hudson's Bay trader remembered selling forty fox traps and one bear trap to a man named Edward Hayward. The numbers coincided with the traps in Charlie King's possession.

Was Edward Hayward the man he called Leaman? The likelihood was strengthened when the register of the Edmonton Hotel revealed the names Charlie King and Edward Hayward entered next to each other on the same date—August 14.

Charlie King had returned to the Lesser Slave Lake settlement with four horses bearing a Diamond C brand. A dealer who had sold them to Edward Hayward was discovered after painstaking investigation.

But no one at Edmonton, apparently, had known Hayward well enough to identify the nugget tiepin, the sovereign case and the silver buckle.

It took Staff Sergeant Anderson, backtracking Hayward through the logging camps of British Columbia, three months to come upon lumberjacks who were able to confirm the three objects as his belongings.

While he was on this quest a middle aged traveler from England arrived at Edmonton. He introduced himself as George Hayward, brother of the missing Edward, before telling his remarkable story to Inspector Strickland.

One night in September George Hayward had dreamed he was in a strange country. He saw Indian tepees and two men on horseback riding by, one of them his brother. The men pitched camp near a slough. Night fell and he saw someone he took to be an Indian woman steal into the camp. While she was there the men began to quarrel. Suddenly the other man seized a gun and fired it at Edward. He fell dead, and the murderer afterwards flung his body onto the fire.

George Hayward brought with him supporting evidence that the dream did occur. Vividly shocked by his experience, Hayward had related it to friends he met at the local tavern next day. A local newspaper had got hold of the story. Hayward showed Inspector Strickland a cutting. The dream had come to him the same night that his brother vanished.

Strickland had an idea. He took the new arrival in Canada to the Fort Saskatchewan penitentiary. Watching a long file of prisoners at exercise, George Hayward suddenly showed great excitement. His trembling finger pointed to a man. He had picked out Charlie King, a man he had seen before just once—in a dream.

When Staff Sergeant Anderson returned and heard George Hayward's story he recollected his first investigation at the camp, and the impression he had had that he was under observation.

He went back to the Cree reservation and, knowing now what had happened, found a girl who admitted having gone to the white men's camp on the fatal night.

Her story tallied with George Hayward's dream. She had run

away when the men began to quarrel, had heard behind her a gunshot and a sudden cry. Fearful of being involved when the Mountie came on the scene, she had sent her brother to watch what he was doing.

The bones which had first made Anderson suspicious and proved on examination to be human, the identification of Edward Hayward's belongings found in the slough, King's attempts to dispose of the traps and the horses—these things built up to a formidable monument of circumstantial evidence.

The dream of George Hayward too added weight. But it was the clue the dream gave, leading to the surprise introduction of the Indian girl into court as a real eyewitness, that became the clinching factor in the case against Charlie King—and gave him a sure ticket to the gallows.

□

CHAPTER FOUR

The Stuff of Dreams Is . . . Murder!

VICTORIAN melodrama is today as dead as Little Willie. But long after ravished maidenhood had breathed a last sigh, wept a final tear, screamed an anguished farewell to the fashionable West End stage, that grand old barnstormer Tod Slaughter kept doomed innocence alive in suburban and provincial halls, where he came round as regularly as Christmas. As genial and gentle a fellow as Santa Claus when you met him privately, Tod leered pure villainy over the footlights, collecting his accolade of hisses annually for half a century before going on to keep his opening date in the Great Elsewhere.

His *pièce de résistance,* to my mind, was *Sweeney Todd, the Demon Barber.* But running it a close second was *Maria Marten: or The Murder in the Red Barn.* Those who ritually shuddered with delight watching this entertainment, were mostly under the impression that the 'orrible atrocities perpetrated nightly by Mr. Slaughter had germinated in the gory fancy of a playwright. 'Twas by no means thus. Maria Marten and company were the truest of true-life characters. Not even the names had been changed to—as they say—protect the innocent. And, villains apart, they were innocents indeed.

The historic story was, of course, straight melodrama. Sometime in the spring of 1827 our heroine, Maria Marten, enticed by her dastardly lover, William Corder, stole away from her parents' rustic cottage at Polstead. They were running off to get married (ha! ha!) at Ipswich—such was the deceitful villain's story.

Well, that was the end of Maria . . . though little did they know it back in the village.

Corder, who managed a nearby farm belonging to his mother, boldly revisited Polstead from time to time. Whenever Maria's father, a sturdy yeoman type, asked after his daughter, the black-hearted scoundrel fobbed him off with assurances that she was well. The snake—scion of landed gentry that he was—must have been a smooth talker. Even the fact that Maria never wrote home—and unlike most girls of her station in life at that time she could pen a readable letter—seems not to have aroused over-much suspicion.

Although Corder himself left the neighborhood for good that autumn, it was well into the new year—ten months after Maria's sudden departure—before family concern rose to the crucial point of taking action.

Mrs. Marten, Maria's stepmother, brought matters to a head by giving her husband the cryptic advice to go take a look at the Red Barn. The structure locally known by that name stood on the farm where Corder had been the manager.

Old Marten naturally wanted to know what reason his wife might have for making this vastly strange suggestion. She told him, explaining that she had hitherto kept silent for fear he would think her superstitious.

Twice, before Christmas, she had dreamed that Maria was murdered and that her body was buried in the Red Barn, "underneath the right-hand bay."

Marten's rustic gullibility, so unfairly matched against Corder's guile, made him still unwilling to do anything. His wife had often dreamed of Maria apparently, and he attached no special significance to these latest sleep revelations, specific and extraordinary though they might be.

Only by continual pressure did Mrs. Marten at last get him to agree to inspect the Red Barn. One can imagine the countless times he must have told her to "stop thy nagging"!

Howsoever slow he was to move, once in motion Marten was sure. He and the man he took along with him, a Mr. William Pryke, were not satisfied by giving the Red Barn a cursory once-over-lightly treatment. A great deal of litter had to be moved aside before they could properly examine the entire floor. They eventually came upon a section which, so they fancied, was not quite so solid underfoot as the remainder. There they started to dig, and found that the earth was, in truth, unexpectedly loose under their spades. At a depth of a foot and a half they struck something soft. It proved to be sacking. Clearing the soil from around it they then saw, pushing through a hole in the sacking, a green silk handkerchief. It was very like the one Maria had been wearing as a scarf when she left home, a gift from William Corder.

After that they were hardly surprised when they uncovered beneath the sacking the body of Maria Marten, betrayed and foully done to death by a scoundrel. His crime brought home to him, Corder confessed, and was meted out his just deserts on the scaffold.*

Stepmother Marten was not the first, and by no means the last, to be vouchsafed a dream solution to a nightmarish crime. Almost contemporary with the Red Barn mystery was a case in Ireland. The workhouse master at Waterford, a man named Burke, disposed of his wife in order to marry a nurse. It was a dream, experienced by the sister of the dead woman, which led the police to investigate. Burke was ultimately found guilty of murder by poisoning and was hanged.

A closer parallel with the Maria Marten affair is to be found almost exactly a hundred years later. One of the original "Big Four" at Scotland Yard, Superintendent Francis Carlin took the leading part in many famous investigations, but never had a stranger introduction to a case than this. It was not heralded by the blast of a policeman's whistle, a gunshot in the night, or the discovery of a brutal slaying. It began officially with a visit paid to Scotland Yard by an elderly clergyman, a person as remote from physical violence as any type of man imaginable. And an equally unlikely choice, one might consider, as a bearer of psychic tidings.

* Many students, in recent years, have come to doubt whether Corder was in fact a deliberate murderer. Maria was not quite the innocent, nor he the cold-blooded villain depicted in traditional portraits.

Nevertheless, the Reverend Gordon Tombe, a Church of England parson, had come to tell Superintendent Carlin about a disturbing dream of murder.

The clergyman nervously explained that his concern was for his son, George Eric Gordon Tombe. Since boyhood Eric had been keen on horses, and while working at the Air Ministry during the first world war he had met a man named Ernest Dyer, who appeared to share his enthusiasm. Together they had raised five thousand pounds when the war ended, and had bought a stud farm—The Welcomes—at Hayes Lane, Kenley, in Surrey.

The previous owner had enjoyed a good reputation as a racehorse trainer, and the venture could have been a success if the partners had pulled together. Unfortunately, Dyer turned out to be more interested in fast cars, and left Eric Tombe, a novice at the job, with the task of training fast horses. Other aspects of Dyer's real character came to be revealed. In his own name only, Dyer insured the farm for twelve thousand pounds, an inflated value on the purchase price. The choice of believing him to be either a lucky prophet or a scheming rogue presented itself forcibly in April, 1921, when a fire of unexplained origin burned down the property in Eric Tombe's absence. The insurance company made its choice plain, as soon as an investigator had made his report, by refusing to pay the claim. Dyer prudently did not take them to court.

This unsavory affair created fresh trouble between the partners; matters continued to worsen until, in April, 1922, a year after the fire, they came to the final break.

Having filled in the background the Reverend Gordon Tombe broached his real cause for worry. Since the partnership was dissolved both men appeared to have vanished. Now, eighteen months after, he still had not heard from his son.

Superintendent Carlin questioned him as to what steps he had taken to inquire. Tombe had information from the bank that checks had been drawn on Eric's account, but could obtain no news from any source of his whereabouts. Unless one considered that a mother's dream could be evidence.

Frequently, the clergyman said, his wife had dreamed of Eric. She believed him to be dead, and that he came back trying to give her a message. In her latest dream—and this was what had persuaded her husband to come for assistance to Scotland Yard —Mrs. Tombe had seen the body of her son lying at the bottom of a well. She felt certain that he had been murdered, and that his purpose in appearing was to tell her so.

Superintendent Carlin asked the question which seemed most relevant: Was there a well on the Kenley farm?

The Reverend Gordon Tombe admitted he did not know.

The Scotland Yard organization was put into motion. Inquiries at the West End bank where Tombe was a customer brought to light a letter received in April (the month the partnership was dissolved) directing that the sum of £1,350 should be transferred to the Paris branch, and that Ernest Dyer should be permitted to draw on it.

The signature on the letter, purporting to be that of Eric Tombe, had been accepted by the bank as genuine. They again had no suspicion when a second letter came in July, by which time Dyer had cleaned out the Paris account, authorizing Tombe's former partner to have power of attorney over the balance —around £2,000—that remained in London. Dyer had emptied this account likewise.

Apart from the bank, the only contact Rev. Gordon Tombe had been able to supply was the address of a girl who had been friendly with the two missing men. Carlin's next step was to interview her.

He was fortunate in striking that rarity, a witness both acute in observation and intelligent.

She told him that Eric Tombe, Ernest Dyer, she and a girl friend, had planned a foursome to go to Paris on the 25th of April. They were to meet at a London railway station, but Eric never arrived. Instead, Dyer turned up by himself and showed the girls a telegram, supposedly from Eric, which said he had been called overseas.

The girl had noticed that Dyer appeared to be hot and nervous. More significant, the use of the word "overseas" in the telegram struck her as strange. Eric, whom she knew well, never referred to "overseas," but always said "France"—or wherever it might be.

She had not heard from Eric since that day. Ernest Dyer, she thought, had gone to the North of England in late autumn that year.

Carlin sent out requests to police forces in the provinces for any information they might have on Dyer. An immediate reply from Scarborough, Yorkshire, gave an unexpected twist to the investigation.

Detective Inspector Abbott, of the Scarborough C.I.D., had had cause to interview a man named Fitzsimmons, who was suspected of passing rubber checks. A newcomer to the well-known seaside resort, Fitzsimmons had also placed a newspaper advertisement inviting men with "ability, highest credentials and sound integrity" to apply for highly rewarding employment, the catch being that a substantial cash investment would be required. It had the hallmarks of a con racket.

Inspector Abbott called at Fitzsimmons' hotel, found him in the bar, and suggested they should go up to his room where he could answer a few questions. Fitzsimmons agreed, and they had reached the landing outside his room when Abbott noticed the man make a surreptitious movement towards his pocket. He immediately grappled with him.

They fell violently, locked together, and struggled on the floor. Suddenly a gun exploded, and Abbott felt the man under him go limp. The bullet, tearing through a vital organ, had killed Fitzsimmons instantly.

The detective was badly shaken. He had not suspected Fitzsimmons of carrying a gun. Even when he jumped the man he had thought he was only attempting to get rid of incriminating documents.

Now the Scarborough police were contacting Carlin because subsequent inquiries had revealed that Fitzsimmons' real name was Ernest Dyer. And among his effects they had discovered personal articles apparently belonging to Eric Tombe, a bag with the initials E. T., and as many as one hundred and eighty blank checks on which Tombe's signature was penciled ready for inking in.

While the Scarborough force believed that Fitzsimmons (or Dyer) had reached for his revolver intending to threaten Inspector Abbott, and had shot himself by accident, Carlin was not so certain. He thought that Dyer, fearing he was about to be charged with the murder of Eric Tombe, might have purposed suicide.

The truth, Carlin decided, could be lying at the bottom of a well . . . at The Welcomes.

He took a team of detectives to the farm. The place was in rack and ruin. The house, never properly restored after the fire, had obviously been evacuated in a hurry. The grounds were overgrown with grass and weeds.

There were no fewer than five wells on the property.

Hefty policemen were set to work clearing away slabs of concrete, brick and rubble. The first well yielded nothing. Neither did the second, and by then darkness had fallen.

The men were hoping to call it a day, but Carlin insisted that they carry on by the light of lanterns. The third well had been filled in with earth on top of the rubble. By the time they got down to water level it was after midnight.

A bucket was lowered. It came up filled with a stinking black sludge. Draining went on until Carlin thought it was time to take a closer look. Letting down a lantern to the bottom he peered over the edge.

The dim rays of light illumined a human foot.

The body they recovered was that of a young man the age of Eric Tombe. He had been blasted in the back of the head by a shotgun.

It was the sad task of the mother whose dream had led to the grim discovery, and the father whose mission it had been to set an official inquiry in motion, to identify the remains of their murdered son.

Although the criminal was beyond arrest Carlin found evidence that supported his theory of the killing and of Dyer's intention to commit suicide if placed in danger of arrest.

The girl who had become suspicious of Dyer at the railway station came forward to say that she had later challenged him with having murdered Eric Tombe before faking the telegram. She had threatened to go to Scotland Yard. Dyer at first agreed to go with her and get the matter cleared up. Then when she picked up a telephone, to call his bluff, he lost his nerve.

If she went to the Yard, he pleaded, he would have to blow

out his brains. The girl dropped the telephone. His scared demeanor convinced her of his guilt, but she did not want to be responsible for his suicide.

Superintendent Carlin traced another witness, Ernest Dyer's widow. She was able to recall a night in June, about two months after the date a coroner's jury settled on as the probable day of the murder, when she was alone at the farm. Dyer was supposed to be in France.

Around eleven o'clock she heard a peculiar noise, sounding like stones rattling against the drainpipe. She went to the door to investigate, and as she opened it saw a figure step out from the deep shadow of the cowshed. It was her husband, Ernest Dyer. She called out, started towards him, but he warned her to get back inside the house.

Dyer had never given her a reasonable explanation for his unexpected and nocturnal visit. Carlin's belief was that Dyer, growing nervous in Paris, came back to fill in the well more thoroughly to guard against chance discovery of his crime.

More impressive from a psychic viewpoint than the Tombe case, though not so difficult for the police once they were brought into it, is the affair of the three friends and the double dream.

Mavis Welch, Myrtle Hughes and Doris Harrison became close friends while working together in a factory at Kilburn, North-west London. For seven years Mrs. Hughes and her husband occupied the ground floor flat in the Harrisons' house at Dagmar Gardens, Kensal Rise, where the Harrisons lived above them. Miss Welch was only a mile away, at Willesden.

In February, 1957, the Hughes family moved to Haywards Heath, Surrey, some sixty miles distant.

Early in June of that year, Myrtle Hughes began to experience a frightening dream. It troubled her for two weeks, and every night it was the same.

She saw in the dream the body of her friend, Doris Harrison, bricked up in an alcove behind a red fireplace. She remembered the fireplace very well . . . it was in the Dagmar Gardens flat where she had lived for seven years.

And she heard the soft, clear voice of Doris Harrison pleading, "Come and find me . . . come and find me."

In the end Myrtle Hughes said to her husband, "I believe Doris has been murdered. I must tell the police."

Bert Hughes scoffed at his wife's foolishness. "You've been reading too many detective stories," he told her.

Undecided about exactly what to do, Myrtle Hughes took a train to London, feeling she had to talk it over with Mavis Welch.

When she arrived she found the other woman as worried as she was. Not having heard from Doris for a while, Miss Welch had thought her friend might have gone to visit her parents in Southampton. Till the night when she too had a dream and heard the voice of Doris begging her, "Come and find me . . . come and find me, Mavis. I'd do it for you."

Fortified by the discovery that their experiences had been so similar, the two women went that same afternoon to Harrow Road police station and told their story.

While not taking the matter too seriously, perhaps, to begin with, the inspector did detail a policewoman to inquire. When she could get no reply to repeated knockings at the Harrison house, detectives were sent to break in.

In the empty flat the Hughes couple had once tenanted they found the body of Doris Harrison in a cupboard under the stairs. She had been battered to death. Beside the body lay a blood-stained tire lever and a hammer.

From the police point of view it was a straightforward case from then on. Detective Inspector Cox soon obtained sufficient evidence to bring a homicide charge against the dead woman's husband.

Frank Harrison was tried and found guilty of murder at the Old Bailey.

The dreams so far referred to have been experiences by relatives or close friends of the murder victims. In other words, a strong emotional link was involved. None of the people concerned was known to be a medium.

Dreams do seem to be a form of psychic experience that comes to people who otherwise are non-mediumistic, and a personal tie between dreamer and subject is common, though by no means essential.

A few years ago the Society for Psychical Research published an account of a precognitive dream of murder. The dreamer knew neither the victim nor the murderer.

Ian Stephens, who contributed this experience to the S.P.R. *Journal,* was a former editor of the *Statesman* of India, Director of Public Information when India was under British rule, and at the time this happened was Director of the Historical Section of the Pakistan Army.

On the night of February 4, 1960, Mr. Stephens dreamed he was in a house, aware of screaming in the fields outside, and "knew it was a murder going on."

He entered a room and saw in front of him a bed "with a living person on it, his feet directed towards me, and not much else of him visible."

He knew that the person in the bed was his best friend, though he did not know the man's identity. Suddenly Stephens realized it was this man, his friend, who had committed the murder outside, and that jolted him awake. The time was 3:15 A.M.

The next afternoon at about 3:30 P.M. Ian Stephens returned from a walk to Flashman's Hotel, where he was living. His orderly, Ali Marjan, greeted him with the news that there had just been a murder in the street outside. Ali Marjan placed the time it happened as 3:15, but later information (Mr. Stephens adds) suggested that it took place a good deal earlier.

Having to go out again, Stephens told his driver to take a route that would avoid the crowds gathered outside the tailor's shop where the murder had taken place. The victim, an employee at the tailor's, had been stabbed by his close friend and first cousin during a quarrel.

However, this establishment was not the one he had supposed, but a smaller shop Stephens had never noticed. So, despite his intention, the route he had directed took him past the premises.

And in a narrow alleyway off the road he saw the dead body of a man lying on a string-bed, his feet towards Stephens, and not much else of him visible.

Ian Stephens, though he might not wish to be described as a medium, confesses he has had other apparently "psychical" experiences. In this present instance the reality next day conformed with his awareness in the dream of a murder taking place out-doors. In dream and reality the positions of bed and body were the same—an interesting detail is that at first the victim's head pointed to the end of the alleyway, according to an eyewitness, but before Stephens passed by the position of the body had been reversed. He surmises that the man's friends may have done this because the alleyway pointed roughly in the direction of Mecca, and it might have been thought disrespectful that his feet should be directed towards the holy city.

In the dream Stephens thought he was looking into a room, but he explains that the construction of the alleyway—an arch conveying the notion of a roof in front, a lower wall at the far end with a high building seen some distance behind—could suggest to someone with poor eyesight, or a dreamer, that he was looking into a long, low room with a half-opened window at the end.

There is an element of distortion present in that it was a dead victim, not a live murderer as in the dream, who occupied the bed. Such reversals or displacements are a baffling feature of many similar experiences.

The account in the S.P.R. *Journal* is offered—with question mark—as an example of linked precognitive dreams. Ian Stephens lays some stress on this aspect.

What happened was that a friend living at the same hotel, Captain Curtis Welborn of the U.S. Army, also had a dream that night and woke up at the same time, 3:15 A.M. Captain Welborn dreamt he was in Korea, where he had served twice, and that a new war was going on. However, none of the features of this dream seems to tally with the actual murder next day. Captain Welborn's identification of the scene with Korea was definite, and he appears to have had only a hazy impression of general-ized violence.

On the other hand, Mr. Stephens saw the man on the bed, knew it was murder, and his strong feeling of friendship, though inaccurately defined, fitted the relationship between victim and murderer.

Apart from the fact that violence was a component of both dreams, and that the times of waking coincided, I can see no reason to connect them. Ian Stephens suggests that he acted in part as a transmitter as well as a receiver, which I find a tenuous sort of argument.

Telepathy between the victim or the murderer and Mr. Stephens would also seem to be an unnecessarily complicated hypothesis. Incidentally, neither Stephens nor Captain Welborn had any acquaintance with the unfortunate pair of cousins.

J. W. Dunne, in his classic work, *An Experiment with Time,* tells of his discovery that a part of our dreams often anticipates future experiences, and the elements of Mr. Stephens' dream appear to be such a foreshadowing of events to come. So the likeliest explanation, I would say, is that Mr. Stephens had a precognitive dream of what his own experience was to be a little more than twelve hours later.

Yet strangers who have no personal involvement, before or after, in the events portrayed in their dream, may find that the experience is entirely relevant. Such a story was told in *Chimes,* the American psychic journal.

Roberta Freiderich was a child, not yet old enough to read newspapers, when in a vivid dream she saw three men walking up the lonely path to a place known locally as Rocky Glen. To her horror she saw two of the men kill the third. They then dug a grave and buried him, pouring what looked like white powder on top of the corpse.

Roberta awoke screaming and ran to her father. After quieting the child he listened to her story. There it might have ended if next morning the newspaper had not reported a man's mysterious disappearance. Mr. Freiderich decided he ought to tell the sheriff about his daughter's dream.

The sheriff knew Freiderich well enough to take him seriously, and sent a deputy out to Rocky Glen. The deputy found a grave, and in it a body on which quicklime had been poured at the time of burial.

Roberta's dream led to the arrest of the murderers. But she herself did not know about that until she was grown up. Then one day, reading a detective magazine, she came across a feature headlined: *Murder Solved by a Child's Dream.*

It was an account of her own experience.

One hesitates to decide what psychic label to attach to such a happening. Mental projection? By what simple or complicated process would a child's mind be drawn to such a scene at such a moment? Telepathy? If so was it between her and the victim, or one of the murderers? An outside intelligence using the child as an instrument of justice? None of these explanations is wholly satisfying.

One remarkable historic example of dreams that are meaningful clearly suggests the reality of telepathic communication from both the living and the dead. The story, told by Cicero in *De Divinatione,* is of two Arcadians traveling together. When they reached Megara one lodged at an inn while the other went to stay with a friend.

The one visiting dreamed that same night that his companion was imploring him to come to his assistance as the innkeeper was about to murder him. He sprang from his bed in alarm, but when he had regained control over himself dismissed the dream as of no importance. He went back to bed and fell asleep. Then the friend appeared to him again, saying that he had been killed, and though it was too late to save him he could still be avenged. The innkeeper had thrown his corpse on a wagon, and covered it with manure. Next morning the cart would be driven through the city gates.

The dreamer, vividly impressed, stationed himself by the city gate early that morning. When the innkeeper came by with his wagon he called on him to halt, demanding to see what was in the cart. The driver jumped down and attempted to flee. Under the load of manure the dreamer found the body of his friend.

Interpreting this we can postulate three possible phases of psychic experience: telepathy between the living at the moment of the crime; telepathy between the dead and the living afterwards; and precognitive awareness of the murderer's plan to dispose of the body—though this last might be accounted for as telepathy between murderer and victim in the first instance.

To return to the present. The war in Vietnam makes private killings there of small significance from the city editor's angle. But in 1960 a Reuters report from Saigon told how a dream led to the solution of an apparently clueless murder. A farmer of Chau Doc province set off from home to sell his buffalo and never returned. Two months later his brother, Tran van Ghan, dreamed that the farmer's ghost appeared and said he had been clubbed to death by two family acquaintances. He told the police and they arrested the two men, who later confessed.

Often these dreamers, bewildered by the strangeness of their experience, say, "I was only dreaming."

And then, sometimes, their dreams come true.

CHAPTER FIVE

□

Dead Men Do Tell Tales

THE name of Charles B. Rosma is not much remembered, even in Spiritualist circles. It ought to be. Speak of the Fox sisters and the response is instant recognition—the founding family of modern Spiritualism, no less! Yet, taking the well-established story at its own evaluation, without Charles B. Rosma there would have been no Fox saga. He it was who broke through to them from the world of the "dead," harbinger of the new revelation.

Charles B. Rosma was a murderee. He had been killed—his story went—in a cottage occupied by the Fox family at Hydesville, New York. Here, tradition has it, Spiritualism was born.

The Foxes moved into their new home on December 11, 1847. The household consisted of John David Fox, his wife Margaret, and their two young children, Margaretta, thirteen, and Catherine, eleven. It was not long before they began to be disturbed by slight movements and knockings in the house at nighttime. At first they thought it was the hammering of a shoemaker who lived nearby.

Soon it became apparent that this could not be the explanation. Besides the knocks there was a tremulous vibration of chairs and beds. Sometimes it sounded as if someone was walking in various parts of the house.

By February the noises had become louder and more varied. So persistent was the nuisance that the Fox family could get no proper rest. Time and again husband and wife took candles and searched every room. The noises went on while they were searching, but they never found the cause.

Now on occasion sheets and blankets were pulled off them as they lay in bed. One night the children felt something heavy lying across their feet. When the youngest girl, Katie, had the sensation of a cold hand moving over her face and was frightened, Mrs. Fox had the children's bed brought into her own chamber.

Near the end of March the phenomena rose rapidly to a climax. On March 30 bangs and knockings resounded through the building all night. When rapping came at a door John Fox would stand before it, ready to fling the door open when the next knock came. However quickly he moved, no one was there.

He had his wife stand guard on the inside while he went to the outside. Rappings then sounded on the door between them.

Margaret Fox had begun to think that the house must be haunted. Next afternoon she confided this belief to her son, David, who lived on a farm a few miles away. He was amused. There must be a simpler explanation than that, he thought. He warned his mother not to mention such a crazy notion to the neighbors.

Friday, March 31, was a day of snow and storm. The family decided to go to bed early, hoping to get a good night's rest. It was a vain hope. This night, though they could never have imagined it, they were destined to be midwives at the birth of a religion.

It began with the usual noises. They had started before Mr. Fox got into bed. The little girls were the mainspring of what then transpired. Grown accustomed to the disturbances, braver now that they were sleeping in their parents' room, they were ready to be saucy. After random knockings had been heard, Katie suddenly called out, "Here, Mr. Splitfoot, do as I do."

She snapped her fingers several times, very rapidly.

Quicker than an echo the same number of raps came in reply.

They were so astonished they could scarcely believe it had happened.

Margaretta was the first to recover. "Now do just as I do," she cried, clapping her hands in time. "Count one, two, three, four."

The rapper imitated her timing.

Katie, taking her turn, made motions with her hand in the air, without any noise. The answering raps were equal in number to her gestures.

"Oh look, Mother," Katie said excitedly, "it can see as well as hear."

The children looked upon it as a game, but the parents were beginning to grow fearful. What seemed akin to a human intelligence was communicating with them, yet . . . there was nobody there.

Katie thought she had found an explanation. "I know what it is, Mother," she said. "Tomorrow is April Fools' Day. Someone is trying to fool us."

Clutching at this idea, Mrs. Fox, intending to put an end to the tomfoolery, if that was what it was, began to ask questions.

"Count ten," she ordered, and the unseen intelligence complied.

"How many children have I?"

Seven raps came. It was a mistake, and for a moment Margaret Fox experienced a surge of relief. Maybe it was just a hoaxer after all. Then she remembered that besides her six living children there was one who had died.

She asked to be given the children's ages. With a pause between each set of raps the correct numbers were given, including the age of the dead child.

As this fantastic quiz proceeded, Mrs. Fox learned that if the answer to a question was negative she got no reply. A flurry of raps meant yes. At her suggestion only two raps came to be sufficient to indicate the affirmative. Before long an efficient, if somewhat laborious, system of question and answer had been established.

By this means she drew from the unseen communicator his claim to be the spirit of a 31-year-old man who had been done to death in that house.

Filled with doubt and wonder, the Foxes at that stage recognized the need for witnesses. John Fox went to fetch their nearest neighbors, the Redfields. When the Redfields had asked questions, and found them being answered correctly, they called in others.

One of the newcomers, William Duesler, had lived in the Fox

house seven years before. He asked if either he or his father had injured the spirit. There was no answer.

Duesler then reversed the question, requesting the spirit to rap if they had not injured him. Everyone heard the raps in reply.

Duesler began to name other tenants of the house prior to the Foxes. Not until he mentioned the name of John C. Bell did the rapper respond.

Step by step—or rather, rap by rap—a story emerged. The communicator declared he had been murdered by John Bell, about five years previously, in the east bedroom of the house. Robbery was the motive. He was carrying with him a trunk and a pack full of merchandise, as well as five hundred dollars in cash. Before nightfall Mrs. Bell, knowing what her husband was about, had gone away with the hired girl. The peddler had gone to bed, and had wakened to find Bell's hands at his throat. He struggled, but Bell overpowered and strangled him. Bell then dragged the body down the stairs to the cellar. The next night he buried it at a depth of ten feet.

After hearing this Mr. Redfield led the way to the cellar. Walking about the cellar floor he asked that a signal should be given when he was standing on the rude grave. At a certain place loud rapping started, then stopped as he moved aside.

In the early hours of the morning, by which time some of the neighbors had gone home, taking with them Mrs. Fox and the two girls, John Fox, his son David, Redfield and others were still questioning the invisible entity. His story never varied, no matter who asked or however much they reversed or changed the wording of the questions.

The most difficult thing was to get his name. It was David Fox who, by calling the letters of the alphabet one by one and waiting for the raps, at last obtained the name C..H..A..R..L..E..S... B... R..O..S..M..A.

The sensation spread next day. Curious spectators thronged the house from early on, but the phenomena did not begin until evening. Hundreds of questions were then asked, and the questioners declared that not a single wrong answer was given. When William Duesler arrived about three hundred people were present. The crowd had grown to five hundred the following day, but except for some responsive raps in the afternoon, when Duesler and others went to the cellar, Sunday passed quietly.

On Monday night David Fox tried to verify that part of the peddler's story which could most easily be tested—the assertion that a body lay buried in the cellar. David and his friends began digging at the spot indicated by the unseen knocker. They soon found themselves in difficulties. The house was on low ground near a stream flooded by winter rains. Water had seeped into the cellar, and they shoveled to a depth of no more than three feet before becoming waterlogged.

It was necessary to wait several weeks for the earth to dry out before another attempt could be made. When they were able to dig deeper they found, among other rubble, traces of charcoal, quicklime, human hair, bones and part of a skull. A surgeon who examined the bones declared they were of human origin.

This partial support for the story encouraged William Duesler to begin a search for people who had lived in the house before 1848. He traced a girl named Lucretia Pulver, who had worked for the Bells in the winter of 1843.

Lucretia remembered a day when a peddler had called, early in the afternoon. Mrs. Bell had seemed to know him and invited him inside. They held a long conversation, and he appeared to be telling her about his personal affairs.

Late that same afternoon Mrs. Bell told Lucretia they could not afford to employ her any longer. She herself was going to spend the night at Loch Berlin, a neighboring village, and if Lucretia would pack her things immediately they could get away together. Mr. Bell and the peddler were alone when the women left.

Lucretia had looked over the peddler's stock earlier on, and had seen several things she would have liked to buy. When she said she had no money with her he had promised to call at her home next morning. He did not come and she never saw him again.

Three days later Mrs. Bell invited Lucretia back to work at the cottage. Soon after her return Lucretia saw Mrs. Bell with two coats she said she was altering for her husband. They were too large for him, she explained, and out of fashion. The garments were unstitched and in pieces when Lucretia saw them.

About this time Mrs. Bell gave her a thimble, saying she had bought it from the peddler.

One day Lucretia had reason to go down in the cellar. Crossing the floor, of a sudden she sank knee-deep into loose earth near the center. Her scream of fright brought Mrs. Bell to the top of the stairs to know what was the matter. Lucretia recovered herself and asked what Mr. Bell had been doing in the cellar. Mrs. Bell laughed away the question. Rats much have been burrowing in the floor, she suggested. A night or two later Mr. Bell carried a load of earth down to the cellar—"to fill up the rat holes."

Several times since her return Lucretia had thought she heard strange noises. Then one night, while the Bells were away at Loch Berlin, she had her little brother and a friend, Amelia Losey, come to keep her company. At midnight, with the little boy asleep, the two girls heard footsteps heavy as a man's walk from the pantry down the cellar stairs . . . and then stop.

Shortly after this Lucretia left her job. She remained on good terms with the Bells, however, and on one of her occasional visits Mrs. Bell mentioned that the peddler had been there again. She showed Lucretia another thimble, and other articles she said she had bought from him.

But even after hearing the story Duesler had to tell, which fitted in well with her own experience, Lucretia was by no means ready to condemn her former employers. She maintained that she had always considered the Bells to be good people, though quick-tempered.

Her mother, Mrs. Pulver, who had often visited the house, even when her daughter no longer worked there, recalled a day when she found Mrs. Bell looking quite ill. Her weak condition, Mrs. Bell said, was for want of rest. Every night and all night long she could hear someone walking about the house, and she was "sick of her life."

The accounts given by Lucretia and Mrs. Pulver lent support to the idea that queer happenings had gone on in the Hydesville house while the Bells were in occupancy.

For the Fox family the hostility and controversy had only just begun. It was never to leave them for the rest of their days.

Katie and Margaretta, around whom the phenomena seemed

to be most active, were taken by their elder sister, Leah, to her home in Rochester. The phenomena pursued them there. Leah moved house three times seeking to escape.

Messages of a prophetic nature started to come through. "You have a mission to perform. Make ready for the work"; "You have been chosen to convince the world"—and suchlike. These persuasions they disregarded for a long while, and to their relief the spirits eventually said they would leave.

The communications did stop for a time, only to return after a few weeks' respite. The sisters were instructed to hire a large hall in Rochester for a meeting. They could hold out no longer. With the help of two friendly clergymen the meeting was arranged, and a committee of well-known people was appointed to test the girls.

To the surprise of their critics the committee made a favorable report. So did a second committee which was elected. A third committee, made up of men who were profoundly hostile, conducted further tests and ended up endorsing the phenomena. The Fox sisters visited other towns, and eventually New York, where Horace Greeley became one of their champions.

The adult history of the Fox sisters is a tragic tale. Margaretta married Elisha Kane, an explorer of good family. She was deeply in love, and when he died a short time after their marriage she never completely recovered from the shock. On top of this were the constant demands made on her to give séances. Her health became overtaxed, and she sought support in alcohol.

Kate went to London and had great success in séances with Sir William Crookes and other investigators. She married a barrister, Samuel Jencken, but this union too was ill-fated. Jencken died soon after the birth of their second child. Katie, like her sister, turned for solace to alcohol.

When drink had deteriorated the strength and character of both Margaretta and Katie, their enemies persuaded them to recant and publicly to denounce Spiritualism. The movement they had unwittingly started had gone too far, and was upheld by too many whose integrity was beyond reproach, for their attacks to do real harm.

The end was near for both sisters. Katie died in July, 1892;

Margaretta nine months later on March 8, 1893. She had re-
tracted her confession before she died.

It is unlikely that anyone except the most die-hard opponent
of Spiritualism takes the Fox confessions seriously. The explanations they gave did little to account for the phenomena so many
thousands had witnessed, including a great many hardened and
skeptical investigators.

Curiously enough, a decade after their deaths, more circumstantial evidence of their initial contact with the spirit world was
unearthed, providing a nicely rounded ending to the story of
Charles B. Rosma. I quote from the *Boston Journal* of November 23, 1904:

> Rochester, N.Y., November 22.—The skeleton of the man supposed
> to have caused the rappings first heard by the Fox sisters in 1848
> has been found in the walls of the house occupied by the sisters,
> and clears them from the only shadow of doubt concerning their
> sincerity in the discovery of spirit communication.
>
> The Fox sisters declared they learned to communicate with the
> spirit of a man, and that he told them he had been murdered and
> buried in the cellar. Repeated excavations failed to locate the body
> and thus give proof positive of their story.
>
> The discovery was made by school children playing in the cellar
> of the building in Hydesville known as the "Spook House," where
> the Fox sisters heard the wonderful rappings.
>
> William H. Hyde, a reputable citizen of Clyde, who owns the
> house, made an investigation and found an almost entire human
> skeleton between the earth and crumbling cellar walls, undoubtedly
> that of the wandering pedlar who it was claimed was murdered in
> the east room of the house, and whose body was hidden in the cellar.
>
> Mr. Hyde has notified relatives of the Fox sisters, and the notice
> of the discovery will be sent to the National Order of Spiritualists,
> many of whom remember having made pilgrimages to the "Spook
> House," as it is commonly called.
>
> The finding of the bones practically corroborates the sworn state-
> ment made by Margaret Fox, April 14, 1848.

Psychic phenomena have been known through the centuries,
but by some quirk of providence, or a method of divine selection
if you wish, it was the outbreak at Hydesville, where the presence of mind of the little Foxes brought about intelligible communication, which sparked off a fire that swept the world.

Discoveries and inventions very often germinate in different minds and different places at about the same time.

Indeed, a little known but strangely parallel case had occurred in England five years earlier. All it lacked was a cute Katie Fox to get on good terms with the rapper!

It happened in a cottage at Chilwell, Nottinghamshire. The main feature of the haunting was violent knocking. The scared tenants called in as witnesses the landlord and his brother. Although intelligible contact was never established the phenomena became so locally renowned that weekend crowds flocked to the cottage. Once or twice railway excursions ran from Nottingham.

Naturally, rumor and speculation had their day. There was a missing peddler, who had last been seen taking a private path which provided a shortcut to the cottage. His disappearance from the neighborhood was puzzling, if only because many of the locals owed him small sums of money he had not gone back to collect.

The tenant of the house fell under suspicion. A witness claimed to have seen him and his son digging in the orchard by lantern light the night after the peddler vanished.

Someone else had overheard the tenant and his wife having an argument. When he threatened her she taunted him, "I could get you hanged any day! I have your coat of arms in the bedroom!"

The meaning of this mysterious warning seems never to have been satisfactorily explained. A possibly bloodstained coat with a weapon in the pocket or wrapped in it is the obvious literal interpretation. But why would the man allow her to keep such dangerous evidence in the bedroom? Why not get rid of it?

When the wife fell ill she died without a doctor being called. Again the rumor was that the husband and the son were frightened that the woman might accuse them on her deathbed.

The most direct piece of evidence came from the tenant's second wife long after. But as she deserted him after sampling the joys of marriage but briefly, her statement could be considered biased. She said: "He used to sit up in bed in the middle of the night, raving, 'There he is! I murdered him! The ax is in the brook!' " True, an ax was found in the brook, but there was never any trace of a murdered peddler.

In the nineteenth century peddlers led hazardous lives. They frequently became the victims of murder and robbery. This was not surprising for they were traveling constantly, mostly in lonely parts of the country, and carrying with them goods and money which made them tempting targets.

One such unfortunate was Murdoch Grant. Instead of following a fixed route, Grant's enterprising policy was to arrive at wedding or funeral feasts where prospective customers, many of them guests from outlying farms, had collected together in goodly numbers.

There was a wedding at Assynt, Sutherlandshire, on March 11, 1830. Murdoch Grant attended and had a profitable day. On taking his farewell he mentioned that he was going to Drumbeg.

About a month later a boy named John Mackenzie, a cotter's son, was strolling along the banks of Loch Tor-na-eigen, not far from Assynt. There had been a drought, and the water was clear and shallow. Not far offshore he saw the outline of a body.

John ran to the village to give the alarm. About fifty people, almost the entire population, went back with him to help drag the corpse out of the water. By some means—said to be the antiseptic properties of a moss growing on the banks of the loch—the body had been kept in a remarkably good state of preservation. Everyone recognized the features of Murdoch Grant.

From the beginning murder was suspected. Grant had a wound in the head, and his peddler's pack was missing. The villagers agreed to submit to the test of touch-proof, a custom then prevailing in Scotland—and a lot of other places. Blood would flow from the corpse, it was believed, at the touch of a guilty party.

One man refused to take part in the ceremony. The village schoolmaster, Hugh MacLeod, disdained such superstition. He was of the opinion anyhow, that there was no real evidence of foul play—the wound could have been caused after death by Grant's head striking a rock.

When the magistrate and the minister arrived on the scene they agreed with MacLeod about the probable cause of the head injury. They were the people in authority, and Murdoch Grant was buried with no more formal inquiry than their brief conference by the loch.

Till weeks later when, as in the best Western tradition, a

stranger rode into town. Actually, Robert Grant is unlikely to have ridden; but he was that excellent plot standby, the brother of the dead man. And Robert was by no means satisfied with the manner of his brother's quick burial. He insisted that Murdoch's body be exhumed.

This in itself accomplished nothing. What made Robert Grant begin to wonder was Hugh MacLeod's persistence in saying that Murdoch must have drowned by accident. This theory hardly explained the disappearance of his pack; still less did it account for no money having been found on the body. Robert became very suspicious that things were not so straightforward as MacLeod was trying to make him believe.

He went on with his inquiries, and no one was more helpful than the village schoolmaster. Then one day a shopkeeper mentioned to Grant an incident of considerable interest: in the shop, that very morning, Hugh MacLeod had dropped his purse, and when it burst open a whole heap of golden sovereigns had rolled on the floor.

A very thought-provoking bit of gossip! Village schoolmasters were not well paid. Robert Grant intensified his inquiries, and learned that MacLeod's fondness for women was costing him more than his salary, and his tastes in living were not cheap. Neither was his reputation for honesty impressive; several times in the past he had resorted to theft in order to pay his debts.

He had MacLeod summoned before the magistrate. When examined, the schoolmaster's replies became so evasive and contradictory that it was decided to arrest him. The official investigation which began where Grant's amateur efforts left off got no further. Something more concrete in the way of evidence was needed if MacLeod was to stand trial.

It came with the appearance of a man named Kenneth Frazer, known in Assynt as "The Dreamer," who had a strange story to tell. His testimony was admitted in court when Hugh MacLeod was tried for the murder of Murdoch Grant at Inverness in September, 1831. This was Frazer's evidence:

"I was at home when I had the dream in the month of February. It was said to me in my sleep, by a voice, like a man's voice, that the pack was lying in sight of the place. I got a sight of the place just as if I had been awake. I never saw the place before, but the voice said in Gaelic, the pack of the merchant is lying in a cairn of stones in a hollow near to their house. . . .

"When the officer came, I took him to the place I had got a sight of. It was on the southwest side of Loch Tor-na-eigen. We found nothing there, and we then went to search on the south side of the burn. I had not seen this place in my dream, but it was not far from the place I had seen in my dream that the things were found. There were five silk handkerchiefs. . . ."

Matching articles were found in Hugh MacLeod's possession.

Strangely enough, while lying in jail awaiting his trial, Hugh MacLeod also had become a dreamer. One night he dreamt he was in a cemetery. An old man was digging a grave. To one side lay an empty coffin.

The grave finished, the old man turned towards him—and to his shock it was his father. "Hugh, here is your grave," his father said. "Lie down in it now, for your time is come."

Panic-stricken, Hugh pleaded with his father, and the ancient relented. "Well, Hugh, go for this time, but remember that in a year your coffin will meet you. Do not forget."

The trial of Hugh MacLeod was postponed from September until the following spring, then again till the next September. He was executed at Inverness on October 24, 1831, before a crowd of about 8,000 people.

On the scaffold he confessed that he had hit Murdoch Grant on the head, robbed him of his money, and had taken some articles from the pack before concealing the remainder "in a cairn of stones"—as seen by Kenneth Frazer in his dream. Later he removed the contents to the place where the officers found them, but whether this was before or after Frazer's dream is unfortunately not recorded.

The natural development in spirit communication after the onset of sporadic rappings was organized séances to receive messages sitting round a table. Dr. Edith Somerville, the eminent Irish writer, was keenly interested in psychic investigation (though critical of the attitudes of some ultraconservative researchers, likening them to weevils nibbling at a biscuit until there was nothing left), and took part in many séances of this kind.

One of the experiences Dr. Somerville attested began with a

Spiritualist group questioning the spirits about a young man who had disappeared in mysterious circumstances.

"Search the river," was the answer they received. A hunt was organized without result.

At the next sitting the same question was asked again, and it got the same response.

The second search ended with the body being found.

At one of the séances the dead man informed them that the murderous attack on him had been witnessed by a nun.

Proof of this statement was long in coming. Finally a nun, who had lived in a convent overlooking the river, confessed before dying that she had watched two men struggling on the river bank, and had seen one throw the other into the water.

At séances today trance communication is in greater favor than table rappings. This form of mediumship offers spirits an opportunity for real loquacity. The messages certainly come through much more speedily; though on the whole not more reliably, I would say.

One of the most abominable murders England has known took place at Eastbourne, a holiday town on the south coast, in the summer of 1920. Irene Munro, a seventeen-year-old Scots girl, went there on holiday, the first time she had been allowed to take a trip by herself. Irene, as the popular description has it, was a nice girl, a typist who had been looking forward all year to her week of freedom by the sea. She may have been ready for a harmless flirtation, but nothing in her young life could have prepared her for the fate she was to meet.

Her body was found on August 20 by a group of children playing on the beach. One child stumbled over something buried in the sand, and they dug to see what it was. To their horror they uncovered a human foot.

This happened on the Crumbles, a lonely stretch of seashore between Eastbourne and Pevensey. Like other natural beauty spots in seemingly peaceful England, the Crumbles has an unpleasant reputation as the scene of more than one murder.

When the police came on the scene and unearthed the remainder of the body, they saw that there were terrible wounds about the head. Pathological examination confirmed first impressions of the cause of death: the girl had been killed by a heavy weight being dropped on her head, repeatedly.

An Eastbourne landlady identified the body as that of her missing lodger, Irene Munro. There were no clues to the identity of her assailants. Irene was a girl who could have had no serious enemies. Neither did she have any friends, at least not in Eastbourne, and a girl alone among thousands of holidaymakers was not likely to be noticed by many.

A well-known London journalist, Harold Speer, was one of the newspapermen working on the case. He decided, other methods apparently getting nowhere, that he might do worse than consult a medium.

The medium he contacted, Miss Groebel, asked if he could make arrangements for her to visit the spot where Irene had died. Speer took her to the Crumbles, late at night when no holiday visitors were around, and there handed her several articles belonging to the dead girl which he had managed to borrow.

In those weird surroundings the medium went into a trance. From her lips came a voice, altogether unlike hers, the voice of a young girl. Irene Munro, whom the speaker claimed to be, begged between broken sobs that her mother would forgive her. She calmed down in a little while, and more coherently told the manner of her death, how the murderers, after knocking her to the ground, had dropped a huge stone on her head deliberately to kill her.

So far it was all known to the police. The medium could have deduced as much from what she had read in the newspapers. But the girl's voice went on to tell more, to describe the two killers. She saw them sitting in the bar of a small hotel in Eastbourne. "It has a white front," she said, "and is called the Albemarle."

Harold Speer passed on to Chief Inspector Mercer the information obtained at the séance. Mercer went to the Albemarle Hotel. It had a white frontage. His questions there put him on the track of Alfred Field and Thomas Gray. Within twenty-four hours he was confident enough of his case to charge them with murder.

When Field and Gray came up for trial at Lewes Assizes the story revealed was that they had met Irene Munro in casual holiday fashion—had picked her up, in fact. They induced her to go for a walk and, as soon as they came to a deserted spot along the Crumbles, attempted to steal her handbag. Irene resisted, and was struck down with a walking stick. While she lay helpless the men took up a large stone and dashed it down on her upturned face, doing it again and again so as to batter her features beyond recognition. After concealing her body in the loose sand they went off with the few pitiful pounds Irene had in her purse. So callous were the precious pair that they went straight to the Albemarle Hotel, squandering the reward of their brutal crime while they flirted with the barmaids.

Taking only an hour to bring in a verdict of guilty against Field and Gray, the jury quaintly added a recommendation for mercy on the grounds that there had been no premeditation. Mr. Justice Avory, a brilliant legal mind, but perhaps also the hardest-headed judge of his day, was hardly the man to support this in any advice he may have seen fit to give to the Home Secretary. Field and Gray were hanged. Those who consider capital punishment a senseless solution might deplore this on general principles, but few murderers have been more deserving of the rope.

This was a period during which the seaside resorts of southern England came out in a rash of homicide. Bournemouth, a little less gaudy than most, is a town favored for permanent residence by retired gentlefolk. Murder intruded upon their calm somnolescence on a day in December, 1921.

The killing of Irene Wilkins, a young servant girl, was elaborately contrived. She was lured to Bournemouth from London by a telegram offering her a situation. Her bogus employer met her at the station, and proceeded with his coldly premeditated plan for murder. Within a few hours of her arrival, Irene Wilkins had been raped and strangled, and her body hidden in a clump of furze bushes.

There were no clues attendant upon its discovery, and for some reason the Bournemouth police did not call in the assistance of Scotland Yard, as the provincial forces usually do in a difficult major case. The investigation dragged on, making little headway.

Then a medium living in nearby Boscombe took the initiative in contacting the police. She had sensed that the murderer was still living in the neighborhood. A visit to the place where the body was found had left her with the feeling that she could be instrumental in his discovery. Unfortunately, her letter offering help was ignored.

Some time later an officer called on the medium about another, quite trivial, matter. They talked about her psychic experiences, and he became so interested that he went back and urged his superiors to give her methods a try. By then they were ready to try almost anything.

Once committed, the Bournemouth police can be given full credit for their determination. It required a whole series of séances with the medium, who sat with a group of other Spiritualists, for all the details of the crime to be disclosed.

The persistence shown by the police in attending multiple séances might be explained by the fact that the first time the medium went into a trance she was controlled by one who convincingly established herself to be Irene Wilkins. Bit by bit, at succeeding séances, they obtained a recognizable description of the murderer, the background to the crime, and even the killer's address.

The police were able to arrest the man, in connection with the issuing of a fraudulent check, and hold him on remand until their evidence was accumulated.

The séances went on while the trial was being held. The spirit of Irene Wilkins uncannily predicted day-to-day progress in court. One witness for the prosecution spoke afterward of his experience in the witness box. Counsel asked him about a material date. He could not bring it to memory. For seconds he hesitated with the court waiting. Then, as if a sheet of paper had been thrust in front of his eyes, he saw in large letters: "January 6." He was convinced that the spirit world had helped him!

Thomas Henry Allaway, found guilty of the murder of Irene Wilkins, was sentenced to death in the courthouse at Winchester. His telltale victim had found a means to expose his calculated plot from beyond the grave. And, twice unlucky, he too had the misfortune to appear before the implacable Sir Horace Avory.

☐

CHAPTER SIX

There's a Good Crime Coming

IF the sterner moralists among us should quarrel with the heading to this chapter, I rest my case with G. K. Chesterton. Illustrating the uses of the word "good," G.K.C., the—in so many ways—outstanding literary figure who created Father Brown, explained that if a man shot his grandmother at a range of five hundred yards he could certainly be called a good shot, but he was not necessarily a good man. On the other hand. . . .

Stephen Foster, not the songwriter but the founder of the London Friendship Centre, told me about an audience he had with Mussolini before the second world war. During their talk it emerged that the dictator, like Foster himself, had occult interests. Mussolini showed him a crystal, which had come from the library of a castle in Italy, and was reputed to be a thousand years old.

Foster, who had some psychic ability, looked into the crystal. So did Mussolini. What the dictator saw were pictures of those Roman emperors who were killed by their own subjects.

"I never saw such fear on a man's face," Foster said to me, "as I saw on Mussolini's that day."

Well, everyone has heard about the fate of Il Duce. And while I am not disposed to argue definitions of "good" as applied to the manner of his going, the world was—if only briefly—a goodlier place at his departure. Maybe "good" riddance is the appropriate salute!

This Mussolini story naturally brings to mind the most famous murder of classical times, the assassination of Julius Caesar. Calpurnia, it will be remembered, dreamt that Caesar fell bleeding across her knees, and warned him not to go out that day. Unheeding he went to the Forum . . . and was stabbed twenty-three times by Brutus, Cassius and the rest.

Premonitions have been prevalent in the history of assassinations. Shortly before King Alexander of Serbia and his wife, Queen Draga, were murdered in their palace in June, 1903, a warning had been communicated to them via a séance room in London.

The message was not forwarded by an unknown correspondent, but at diplomatic level. In fact, by the king's own Ambassador to the Court of St. James, Count Myatovitch. Both he and the young heir to the Serbian throne had been present at the séance.

The story came to me from Dr. Flora Ames, president of the Medical Botany Union, after she read a piece I had written on a much later séance at which Count Myatovitch conversed with Queen Draga in their own tongue through the Welsh medium, Evan Powell.

Dr. Ames recalled an evening in 1903 when she was invited to the home of W. T. Stead, the distinguished London editor. Among the guests was Mrs. Burchell, a medium from the north of England. After dinner Stead suggested holding a séance.

Count Myatovitch handed the medium an envelope containing a letter he had received from King Alexander, written in his own language. The moment Mrs. Burchell took it in her hand she gave an exclamation of horror.

She said she could see the king, whom she described, in a room at the palace. The queen was with him. Suddenly a man rushed in and attacked them—and the medium went on to give a graphic, and what later proved a true, account of the assassination.

Another of the guests, claiming also to have a vision, mentioned the entry of guards in "Russian" uniforms. Serbian and Russian uniforms at that time were very similar.

That same night Count Myatovitch dispatched a warning to the king by diplomatic courier that an attempt on his life would be made. It did not prevent the assassination at Belgrade shortly afterward.

There was an interesting sequel. When news of the murders reached London a publisher asked Dr. Ames to write the royal love story for early publication. With the help of Myatovitch, who lent documents and photographs, Dr. Ames, in a tremendous burst of effort, quickly completed the manuscript. She then found herself stuck for a title.

She was resting in her sitting room when a woman dressed in a pink evening gown came from a corner of the room towards her. Three bloody fingermarks were imprinted on her pale cheek. In a low voice she said, "Call it *The White City of Death.*"

The vision faded. "But the memory was too vivid to be forgotten," said Dr. Ames, "and the book was published under that title."

When fuller reports of the assassination reached London it became known that Queen Draga had been wearing a new pink dress from Paris the night she died. The murderer had left a bloody imprint of three fingers on her face.

Political assassination has been rare in Britain. Guy Fawkes, who tried it on a big scale, failed in his attempt to blow up the whole Parliamentary caboodle. He is still burnt in effigy every November 5 by the law-abiding British, though why he should for so long be execrated and unforgiven for his failure is slightly puzzling.

The precincts of Parliament have not been kept entirely remote from murder. A Chancellor of the Exchequer, Spencer Perceval, was assassinated in the lobby of the House of Commons—not on account of his tax policies, incidentally, for the murderer, John Bellingham, was declared to be a madman.

A few days prior to the attack, Mr. J. F. Williams, the manager of a copper mine at Redruth, Cornwall, had three times experienced an unusual dream. He saw the scene in the lobby of the House as a man shot the Chancellor with a pistol. The Chancellor fell, with blood gushing from his chest. So plain was the vision that Williams could afterwards state the number of buttons on the assassin's coat, and the color of them. His account of the dream is preserved in the British Museum.

Another English assassination which caused a stir towards the close of the nineteenth century was also previewed by a dreamer. The victim was William Terriss, a matinee idol who in popularity ranked higher than Irving, Beerbohm Tree or Martin-Harvey. He was stabbed as he entered his private door at the Adelphi Theatre in the Strand.

The night before, an actor named Lane, who was appearing in the play with Terriss, dreamed what was going to happen. He saw Terriss lying bleeding on the steps inside the door, with the company standing around him, Lane himself among them. He watched Terriss die in the arms of his son-in-law, the young actor who was later to become Sir Seymour Hicks.

Lane was so disturbed next day by his memory of the dream that he told other members of the company about it. They treated it lightly, as nothing more than an alcoholic aftermath.

Until a while later when Terriss, arriving at the theater, was ambushed by a madman in the alley just as he was opening his private door. The famous actor was carried inside to die . . . and Lane saw his dream scene enacted in reality, himself part of the group standing exactly as he had seen them in his vision less than twenty-four hours before.

I heard from W. Macqueen Pope, famous historian of the London theater, a story suggesting that the ghost of William Terriss was seen just a few years ago.

A man walking down the alley beside the Adelphi stepped aside to make way for an impressively handsome figure, dressed in old-fashioned clothes, to go past him. His curiosity aroused, the man turned for a second look at the stranger. The figure had vanished . . . at the door Terriss had so often entered to meet public acclaim and, finally, his assassin.

The witness, Pope said, knew nothing about the Terriss tragedy until he happened to mention his experience to a friend connected with the theater. Other stories of Terriss's alleged manifestations have come to me, none of them carrying much evidence of identity. But, traditionally at least, William Terriss is numbered among the many ghosts of London's haunted theaterland.

Warnings which come to people not directly involved in the projected tragedy seldom achieve their purpose—if their purpose is to prevent. Even when it is possible to pass on the warning it is mostly ignored. The price of proof is failure in this sense, it would seem, for if a crime is prevented from taking place the prevision of it cannot completely come true.

People often do act on premonitions in matters of life and death not connected with crime. But when it comes to murder most people have difficulty in believing it could ever happen to them. Then there are instances of clear warning, sensed directly by the coming victim, who has failed to take evasive action owing to circumstance or the persuasions of others.

Robert Galemont, driver of a French postal service van, one day said to a friend and fellow worker, "If ever I am killed it will be here." They were driving along a section of Galemont's route, a bleak and lonely stretch of road in Arras.

A while before, their conversation had touched on the risks run by drivers of bank and postal lorries from gangs of robbers. But no holdups had occurred in their region of France, and neither Galemont nor his friend had immediate cause for anxiety. So the other man asked, curiously, "Why do you say that?"

"I say it," Galemont replied, "because the very first time I came on this route I felt a cold shiver of horror when I reached this point. I have never passed here since without that feeling having returned."

This conversation took place during the early part of 1950. Over a year later Galemont's dead body was found at the place he had indicated to his friend. His many wounds gave evidence of his desperate struggle to defend the mails in his charge before his attackers succeeded in strangling him with a bicycle chain. The postal sacks had been ripped open and looted.

Galemont was last seen alive by the driver of a lorry which passed him going in the opposite direction. He told the police that sitting beside Galemont in the driving cab was a stranger in a beige mackintosh, to whom he was apparently giving a lift. The police gathered evidence pointing to this man having acted as decoy for one of the gangs perpetrating the wave of similar crimes in other parts of France.

My other story from France had its start a year after Galemont's presentiment of violent death had come true, when M. Henri Gony, a prosperous printer, took his wife to see a plot of land he had recently inherited. It was situated a few miles from Paris, in a pleasant suburb, and M. Gony was both shocked and disappointed when his wife at once declared, "I refuse to live here. If I do I shall be murdered!"

Of course, he tried to argue her out of what he called superstitious notions. Being a good husband, however, he did not persist too much in the face of her obvious distress.

But he did not relinquish his plan entirely. The administration had marked the area that included his land as the site for a model residential section attractively named Bois Fleuri. In M. Gony's estimation it would be a most desirable place to live. So after giving the matter some thought he offered his wife a compromise. Instead of building a single house he would put up three cottages. Two could be rented out, and with neighbors so close she need have no fear of being alone and unprotected while he was at business.

After a certain amount of hesitation Madame Gony agreed. M. Gony forthwith consulted his architect, and then began to build. The cottages were ready to move into by the summer of 1955.

Everything went well from the very beginning. Madame Gony became an enthusiastic gardener, her former fears seemingly forgotten. Her husband and their only son, Philippe, who when his job at Le Bourget airport allowed visited them on Sundays, could even tease her about her superstitions without upsetting her unduly.

Then one day in October, Henri Gony, home early from work, was surprised not to see his wife out in front tending her flowers as usual. It was still broad daylight, and there was really no cause for alarm. Yet something made Gony recall his wife's premonition. His unease grew profound as he walked up the garden path, and became apprehension when he found the front door locked and could get no answer.

M. Gony went round the back to the kitchen entrance . . . and there came upon the body of his wife, brutally struck down with her own garden spade. Robbery had been the motive, the killer having ransacked the house.

After the murders of Jack the Ripper the most sensational criminal activity that the East End of London can boast is the outbreak of gang violence which culminated in the notorious Siege of Sidney Street. Winston Churchill, who was then Home Secretary, not only called out a company of Scots Guards from the Tower of London, but went himself to direct the onslaught against the terrorists, ordering a cannon and a troop of Royal Horse Artillery as reinforcements.

It started with the murder of three unarmed policemen by a gang of safe breakers. The English burglar of the period, caught in the act, more often than not "came quietly." If cornered he might try to give a policeman a bashing with his fists, or even go so far as to use a blackjack. But violence on this scale by the professional thieving classes was unprecedented. It smacked of something foreign. And foreign it was, literally.

The murders took place in Houndsditch. It is a surprise to most people to learn that the authority of the Metropolitan Police, with headquarters at New Scotland Yard, does not extend to a vital part of London—the City itself. The financial heart of the metropolis covers little over a square mile, but it houses the Bank of England, the Stock Exchanges, the head offices of nearly all the main banking and commercial institutions . . . and has its own police. Houndsditch is on the borderline between the two territories, and both the Metropolitan Police and the City of London Police were deployed on this case in full strength.

The night of the murders Detective Sergeant Lawrence Seal was one of the hundreds of policemen who were out on the street seeking a lead to the hiding place of the criminals. Seal was better placed than most to gather information. A member of the Special Branch, which deals with political suspects, he had been living as a down and out in a common lodging house at Shadwell, keeping an eye on members of a Russian Nihilist organization.

That night Seal met one of his contacts, a man talked about in the district for his psychic ability. Seal, only half in earnest, asked him if he had any psychic help to offer the police on the Houndsditch murders.

The man said he thought he might if he could have contact with something the criminals or the victims had handled.

Seal hesitated, then remembered the man's local reputation, and decided to take him seriously.

He was able to borrow an empty cartridge clip case found at the scene of the crime. The psychometrist took it in his hand, and almost at once became greatly affected. In a state of trance he began to talk in a deep voice contrasting with his ordinary high-pitched tone.

There was a house, he said, within a mile of where they were standing. In one room were two men and a woman. In another room, where it was dark, was a blood-soaked bed, and lying on it a dead man. Coming towards the house, but still a long way off, was a man with a drooping black moustache.

Then the vision moved on to a second phase . . . The two men were gone from the room. The man with the moustache had reached the house. He was inside, looking down at the dead man on the bed. He bent down and took something from underneath the pillow.

And the third phase . . . Two men in a dark room—noises—crowds—flames—and policemen carrying coffins.

All this proved to be an accurate foreseeing of the sequence of events next day.

Frederick Wensley, then holding the rank of Inspector, but later as Superintendent to become one of the original "Big Four" at Scotland Yard, and later still, Chief Constable of the C.I.D., at that time wore a drooping black moustache. It was he who entered the house at 59 Grove Street—less than a mile from where the medium was when he had his vision—and there found the dead murderer, Gardstein, also known as Morountzoff, lying on a bloodstained bed. Beneath his pillow was an automatic with one bullet missing from the clip—which was identical with the empty case clip handled by the medium. In another room a woman accomplice, Sara Rosa Trassjohnsky, was caught while burning papers.

The men who got away sought refuge in a house at 100 Sidney Street. Pursued there they refused to surrender, and the house was besieged by police and military. By some means the building caught fire, and the killers chose to die in the flames rather than surrender. Their charred bodies were afterwards removed in coffins by uniformed policemen.

Serious students of the occult—those who take themselves seriously, anyway—usually tend to frown on teacup reading. True, ninety percent or more of it may well be nonsense. Anyone can amuse himself finding shapes in the tea leaves and imagining they must mean something. For the real clairvoyant, however, the tea leaves merely act as a focal point of concentration; and for that purpose can serve as well as any other means. Much in the same way that, given the talent to paint, the canvas, wood or other base used is a matter of choice or circumstance. Without the talent, messing about with paintbrushes can provide a lot of fun, but the result won't be a masterpiece.

Chief of Police Joe Doran was a hard-bitten Irish cop who thought all forms of fortune-telling were strictly for the dodos. Therefore, when one of his men, Walter J. Macy, later a Superintendent in the San Diego Police Department, walked into headquarters with a fantastic story to unload, he did so in greater fear than he had ever known when walking into tong battles amid whirling knives and meat cleavers.

It had taken Macy half the day to summon up his courage. Up to the night before he had been as big a scoffer as his chief. He knew just how Doran would react. Nevertheless, he had a compulsion that could not be denied.

It helped not at all when Doran, taking one look at Macy's expression, asked him if he had seen a spook. So near the bone was it that Macy blurted out everything in a rush to get it over.

There was going to be an armed robbery on Sunday night, he told Chief Doran. One man, a civilian, would be shot, literally full of holes. A businessman would be killed also. A police officer in uniform, wearing black boots—a motorcycle cop by the description—would be badly shot up. He didn't know whether the policeman would die. He didn't know where the robbery would be.

Chief Doran stared at him popeyed when he finished. Then, with an effort, he summoned enough control to ask Macy where he got his information.

Nervously, Macy told him. The night before—May 4, 1928—on the way home from headquarters, he had called to pick up his wife, who was visiting a close friend, Mrs. Myrtle Hoffman.

At Mrs. Hoffman's home on Marborough Avenue he had been invited to have a cup of tea. Then Mrs. Hoffman offered to read his tea leaves. This was a big joke to Walt Macy, but he went along with it. Mrs. Hoffman, a lively, laughing person, did not mind his teasing threat to arrest her. For his part he did not want to be a spoilsport. It was just a game.

But it turned to grim drama when Mrs. Hoffman described the clairvoyant picture she saw. Her intensity, her conviction of truth, sent a chill down the spine of a man who after sixteen years on the force was adept at reading the faces of witnesses of all types. She had told him what he had just passed on to Chief Doran. It went against all his convictions, he hadn't believed her, wouldn't allow himself to . . . but he was so shaken he just had to do something about it.

Chief Doran could not be expected to take it as seriously. After all, he had not been there. He told Macy to forget the whole thing, and he would do the same. Macy went home and spent a miserable weekend imagining the cruel ribbing he would get from his colleagues if the tale leaked out.

On Monday morning, reluctant as he was to face them, he nevertheless got down to headquarters early . . . and found an unshaven Chief Doran impatiently waiting for him at the top of the steps.

Macy barely had time to notice the unusual activity going on in the detective bureau for that time of day before the chief had him in his office and was barking questions. Who the hell was this tea leaves woman? How well did he know her?

Macy muttered that Mrs. Hoffman had been a family friend for fifteen years. She was completely trustworthy. Then Chief Doran told him what had happened.

Sunday night two men had held up the California Theater. The manager, James F. Malloy, was shot dead. Two motorcycle cops spotted the getaway car and went in pursuit. One of them, Archie Comstock, got knocked off his machine by a bullet when he tried to run the holdup car into the curb. He was seriously, but not fatally, wounded.

The stickup men had abandoned their car near First Avenue Canyon. Police and sheriff's men followed a trail of blood that led them to a house on the canyon rim. The trail ended at a cellar door stained with dripping blood. When the officers called on the fugitives to come out they got no answer. Detective Sergeant Hugh Rochefort and Deputy Sheriff Blake Mason, both carrying sawed-off shotguns, were the first to go in. The beams of their flashlights circled the cellar. As they were moving toward one end they heard a slight noise behind them. Wheeling round they saw the foot and lower leg of a man just visible, the rest of him hidden behind a brick chimney. Both officers fired and the man stumbled forward. They fired again. He crashed to the floor, riddled with shot.

The man peppered like a sieve proved to be Otto Andrew Morrissery, an ex-convict from Long Beach, California. He was not the killer of Malloy. His homicidal partner, identified by witnesses having noted that he had letters or figures tattooed on the back of his fingers, was James Durant, alias Ralph Hill. It took five years to catch up with him. Durant was picked up for a store theft at Logan, Utah, in March 1933, and returned to San Diego to face the felony charge. His plea of guilty to murder and attempted armed robbery drew him a life term in Folsom. An ironical touch —the letters tattooed on Durant's fingers formed the words, TRUE LOVE.

Long before this a converted Chief Doran had released the story of Mrs. Hoffman's part in the drama to the newspapers. Maybe she would have preferred him to remain skeptical of her abilities, for the result was a rush of people wanting her to peep into the future on their behalf.

Inspiration may follow a cup of tea more often than one would suppose. Dr. John Glaister, Emeritus Professor of Forensic Medicine at Glasgow University, and one of the great medico-legal experts, recalls the instance of a woman found naked and dead under the bed in her apartment.

Two women in Glasgow visited a fortune-teller. They were worried about their married sister because, contrary to her custom, she had not been round to their mother's home for two successive days.

The woman, gazing at the tea leaves, said: "I can see police in the cup. I'm afraid the worst has happened to your sister. You should go to her house and make a thorough search—and don't forget to look under the bed."

As Professor Glaister, in his book *Final Diagnosis*, himself comments: "An extraordinary start to any investigation. . . ."

The woman had died of asphyxia caused by a scarf knotted around her neck. But it was tied in such a way that to decide between murder and suicide was impossible. In an experiment fifty men and fifty women were asked to tie the same kind of knot, first as they would if they were tying a scarf around their own neck, then as if tying it around the neck of another person. The results showed no difference in the shape and positioning of the knots to indicate suicide or murder. The case was never resolved, though Glaister had his own opinion.

Flagrant miscarriages of justice have occurred at times by reason of corruption, prejudice or plain human error. Even when no one else is disturbed, the victim certainly knows all about it. Yet one man in the Connecticut State Prison a few years ago did not know himself if he had done the killing for which he was sentenced.

His story was told in *Fate* magazine, but because of current efforts to free him certain details were withheld and the prisoner was identified only by the initials, D.H.B.

In July, 1953, D.H.B. was working as dispatcher for a shipping company at Hartford, Connecticut. One day his boss asked him if he would like to become manager of the new terminal to be opened in a neighboring city. Even in his eagerness to grab the opportunity, D.H.B. had a queer feeling that he would never take over the job.

That same night he had a dream. He knew it was Saturday afternoon, and he saw himself sitting in a movie theater. Only the strange thing was that the theater was inside a prison. All around him were convicts, whose faces were unfamiliar. At that time he knew so little about prison conditions that on waking he wondered whether inmates were ever allowed movie shows.

On leaving work the next Friday, D.H.B. had another uncanny experience. An "irresistible force," as he described it, pulled him away from the route he had been taking every day for two years. Entering a side street he went into a bar, and ordered whisky with a beer chaser. He knew that the bar was new to him, yet he had the feeling of having been there before. He had drink after drink, in what seemed like a trance, before leaving and going to another bar across the street.

He had no recollection of what happened for two days after that, when he found himself telling a lawyer that he had killed a woman, but he did not know her name or where the body was.

The lawyer took him to the police. They knew nothing about

a murder. A police surgeon was brought in to examine him. He suspected that D.H.B. was a psychiatric case, and sent him to a hospital for observation.

Next day the police came for him. The body of a woman had been found. According to his story the police got him to sign a confession, then charged him with first degree murder. The grand jury indicted him for murder in the second degree. When his trial came up he was allowed to plead guilty to manslaughter, and was given a ten-to-thirteen year sentence.

So it came about that, soon afterwards, he was sitting in a prison theater on a Saturday afternoon, watching a movie with other convicts. His dream had come true.

Up to now, taking D.H.B.'s story at face value, we have to consider not only the precognitive dream, but also his state of mind on the night he lost his memory. A sequel two years later widens the range of speculation considerably.

In June, 1955, a former colleague at the freight company confessed to two fellow workers that he had killed the woman for whose death D.H.B. had been held responsible. Soon after this the man was found drowned in only two feet of water, a circumstance implying the possibility of foul play.

The problem is fascinating. Was the colleague guilty? If so, did he commit suicide, or was he put out of the way by an accomplice? Did D.H.B. kill the woman in a state of amnesia? If so there is the coincidence of two men of abnormal mentality, linked together by their employment, confessing to the same crime.

Or do we need to seek a more devious explanation? Spirit possession is a theory which would account for D.H.B.'s strange condition on the night of the killing. Hypnosis is another, either as a means of making him commit the crime, or making him confess falsely to having done so.

In this present case there is not sufficient evidence to prove or disprove any hypothesis. All one can say is that D.H.B. apparently had a precognitive dream, which was not specific enough to be of the slightest help as a warning.

Psychic experiences are often like that.

□

CHAPTER SEVEN

Murderers from Hell

BEFORE children can give evidence in court the judge has to be satisfied that they understand the nature of the oath (though many adults never consider its full implications). Fulfilling his judicial duty, Mr. Justice Maude asked a little girl:

"What do you suppose will happen if you don't speak the truth?"

The child spoke up confidently.

"I shall go straight to hell."

"Swear her," ordered the judge. "She knows much more than I do."

More than most of us. Even if she was not quite so knowing as the other child who, replying to the same question, said brightly, "My witness expenses won't be allowed."

A century before the instance I have mentioned, a young brother of Maria Marten was called to give evidence at William Corder's trial. He was asked by Lord Chief Baron Alexander if he knew what would happen to him should he swear falsely. He too replied, "God would send me to hell, sir."

While it is impossible to believe with the fundamentalists that untruthful children are disposed of so arbitrarily, that does not refute the idea that hell exists.

The modern theological view that hell is a state of mind makes it none the less real. And it follows, once we accept the notion that certain discarnate spirits may contact us as messengers of light, that others may attempt to do so with darker intent.

The vicar of a Yorkshire parish climaxed a most unclerical career by gassing himself. He had never held benefices for long because of his "diabolical" temper, was known to have "fiendishly" mistreated his own small children, and had a passion for laying curses on all who offended him—adopting the mocking posture of administering a Christian blessing while so doing. At the inquest the coroner said that the letters the parson had left behind were too horribly vindictive to be read, though there was much evidence attesting to his sanity. The jury declared, "In our opinion the vicar was possessed of an evil spirit at the time of his death."

This was in the nineteen-thirties. Even at that date the jury could be considered old-fashioned in their ideas. Although for many centuries every human ill was ascribed by the learned to its cause, demonic possession has gone out of tune with the times. A rational approach was sorely needed, but the result has been to throw out the baby with the bath water. More aptly maybe, the demon was thrown out with the holy water.

The Bible retains its reports of the casting out of devils. No one has got around to expurgating them yet! But very few Protestant bishops unequivocally subscribe to such beliefs. Psychiatrists, too, prefer other labels for all the baffling abnormalities they encounter. This leaves Roman Catholics and Spiritualists as the main groups who—from different angles of approach—are still willing to accept possession by evil spirits as a reality.

As David Hume put it, "The Catholics are better believers than the Protestants because they have in their history of saints so many spirit manifestations." Rome wisely follows St. Paul in rating charity above the possession of psychic gifts. Nonetheless, two miracles before the death of the candidate are the minimum for beatification, and two more must follow after death before sainthood can be pronounced. The tests are strict by any standards. It has been well said that "it takes a miracle to prove a miracle to Rome." Since the sixteenth century, priests inquiring into cases of alleged possession have been taught to exclude melancholia, lunacy and suggestion before making an attempt at exorcism. Evidence of secondary personality and xenoglossia (speaking in tongues) is admitted as possibly indicating possession.

Trance control, as known to Spiritualists and others, can be very simply defined as possession by a discarnate spirit. The differences between this form of mediumship and demonic possession are not technical, but moral: "By their fruits ye shall know them." Trance control is undertaken with the consent of the subject, respect for the individuality of the instrument is maintained, and outside the period allowed for the experiment there is no interference with normal life. No dissociation or disintegration of personality is involved. After a short spell of voluntary abeyance for the control to operate, the medium's self is able to resume full authority. The purpose is benevolent.

Demonic possession has the same *modus operandi*. But it is achieved without the consent and often, though by no means always, against the wishes of the involuntary medium. It commonly assumes an obsessional nature that persists in the waking state. In fact, the obsessional aspect is probably much the more frequent, states of deep trance seldom being realized.

Allow the hypothesis that states of possession and obsession can exist, and the possibility of crimes being induced or controlled by evil spirits presents itself immediately.

Some places, cliffs, ponds, rivers, offer themselves as natural spots for suicide. Why the same section of a cliff, one particular pond or stretch of river, should be chosen repeatedly is not clear.

Sir Shane Leslie, in his ghost book, tells of a haunting at an English country house. In the earlier stages the witnesses were not aware that others had experienced anything out of the ordinary. Leslie had been able to question some of them, and had seen the complete dossier of statements by all. The entire range of phenomena, says Shane Leslie, a Catholic authority on psychic manifestations, suggests "an authentic intervention in human affairs by a spirit, and an evil one at that." I need refer to only one incident.

An army officer, visiting over the weekend, put out his light on getting into bed, and immediately felt the sensation of fingers stroking his face. He thought it a delusion, but nevertheless switched the light on again. No one was there. He turned off the light—and experienced the same sensation. When it had happened a third time he searched the room, found no intruder and, not really alarmed but certainly wide awake, decided to read a book. He found it impossible to concentrate. Horrible thoughts began to enter his mind, followed by a feeling of despair and an urge to kill himself. He had no reason at all to be contemplating suicide. Nonetheless, his mind began to dwell on the pond in the garden, which he had scarcely noticed when he arrived. The compulsion became irresistible, and in a moment he was climbing out of the window to get to the pond the quickest way. Then suddenly the pressure was removed. So weak and shaken was the officer after his experience that the only desire he had was to get away from the house. He departed before breakfast, leaving a note of lame apology for his host.

The servants were told nothing of this and the unpleasant experiences other visitors had undergone. Yet some while later a maid, in the middle of cleaning out a room, put down the brush and dustpan, walked out of the house, and threw herself into the pond. No motive for her wanting to kill herself could be produced at the inquest.

Later still a search was made at the Public Records Office. It was discovered that since the reign of James I a great number of suicides had occurred in or near that pond. They took place in batches, separated by irregular periods when nothing happened, the longest such interval being about sixty years. Some unfortunates had jumped in the water, others had hanged themselves on trees near the verge, and a farmer had walked eight miles from his own farm to shoot himself by the pond.

The famous French astronomer, Camille Flammarion, told the somewhat similar story of a woman who became obsessed with the desire to throw herself from the window of one particular room in her home. So strong did the impulse become that she was forced to move house. Unknown to her then, the wife of the previous owner had committed suicide by jumping from the window to which she was so impelled.

Then there is the story of the police cell at the Fourth Precinct Station in New Orleans, where a number of prisoners have tried to hang themselves, so it is alleged. One girl, Mary Naylor, was saved at the last minute. She said an old woman had appeared to her and urged her to hang herself from a bar of the cell window. She tried to resist, but finally the influence overcame her. The description Mary Naylor gave matched the appearance of Ann Murphy, who had succeeded in hanging herself in that cell long previously.

And so to murder. . . .

Before his execution Franklin B. Evans, killer of a twelve-year-old child, confessed: "For some days before the murder I seemed to be attacked continually by one who seemed to bear a human form, urging me on to the deed. At length it became fixed in my mind to take her life."

There is the curious case of Peter Kuerten, Germany's Jack the Ripper, who was bloodthirsty in the most literal sense. Kuerten was a middling man in every respect—age, build, looks and personality. An inoffensive, colorless artisan anyone would have thought him. Most of the time he was! Kuerten was married, and again, his wife got along with him middling well, though she found him moody at times.

The bloodlust came upon Kuerten at varying intervals. In two years of terror, 1929 and 1930, he accounted for at least a dozen victims of both sexes. The police suspected he had done more than twice that number of killings. Kuerten himself could not remember. When opportunity allowed he buried his bodies in a convenient field or patch of shrubbery on the outskirts of Dusseldorf. Some of his victims may still be lying in undiscovered graves.

Shortly before he was apprehended Kuerten confessed everything to his wife. She had never suspected his activities. Her mind gave way under the shock, and she had to be put in an asylum. "I kept everything from her for as long as I could," Kuerten said. "I did my best not to hurt her." He seemed almost grateful to the police. "If you had not arrested me when you did," he said, "I know I would have had to take another life."

Kuerten's first known killing took place in 1926. An American, uncle of the child victim, was charged with the crime. He was later released, his innocence established. But it was not until 1929 that the police, searching for the knife used on one victim, stumbled across Kuerten's field of death where other corpses were buried. Only then did Dusseldorf become aware that a mass murderer was loose in the city.

The police visited a medium, Frau Lotte Plaat, and asked her to hold a séance. What they hoped for was a clue to put them on the track of the killer. What they got was the spectacle of a medium controlled by an entity so apparently evil as to gloat over the criminal's success in evading capture.

"I control him," the spirit boasted. "He does what I command. When I want blood he drinks it for me. You shall not take him. He is mine."

It was a fact that Kuerten drank from the bleeding wounds of his victims. Other séances maintained the same pattern, alleging that Kuerten was a man possessed. The theory became horribly persuasive when the compulsive nature of Kuerten's acts was established.

The fairy story began when Evelyn Nesbit came from Pittsburgh to New York, a penniless and (possibly) innocent girl. At sixteen Evelyn was a member of the *Floradora* chorus and the mistress of a millionaire—Stanford White, one of America's three foremost architects. At nineteen Evelyn left White to marry a multimillionaire—Harry Thaw, heir to Pittsburgh railroad millions. Before she was twenty-one Evelyn had become the apex of America's most celebrated triangle murder. Midnight had struck for the Pittsburgh Cinderella!

Oscar Wilde, on being asked by the United States Customs if he had anything to declare, riposted, "Nothing except my genius." Stanford White, if he got to the gates of heaven, could have borrowed the quip. Maybe St. Peter would add to the balance a degree of kindness White had shown to the girl he seduced. About the nicest thing to be said in favor of Harry Thaw is that much of the blame for his shortcomings could be laid at the door of his progenitors. Both men were indulgent to their vices above all else.

On June 25, 1906, Harry and Evelyn, with two male guests, went to the opening of *Mam'zelle Champagne* at the dining theater on the roof of Madison Square Garden. At a nearby table, alone, sat Stanford White.

The show did not come up to expectations. One number had the somewhat provocative title *I Challenge You to a Duel*. It was soon followed by a ballad, even more pointed perhaps to a few members of the audience, *There Was a Maid*. The leading man, Arthur Sandford, had not finished this last song when Harry

Thaw took steps to liven up the entertainment. He walked over to Stanford White, raised a pistol, and fired three shots. White fell to the floor with two bullets through his brain. Thaw changed his grip on the smoking gun, holding it by the muzzle as if to demonstrate that he meant no harm to anyone else.

The case was open and shut on the face of it. Harry Thaw was taken to Center Street, charged with murder in the first degree, and carted off to the Tombs. Back in Pittsburgh bookies were soon offering four to one on his getting the electric shock treatment at Sing Sing. Worldly-wise New Yorkers stuck by the saying, "You can't electrocute a million dollars."

Seven months later when the trial opened, the battery of legal talent hired to defend Harry Thaw had decided, after some disagreements and withdrawals from the case, to enter a plea of guilty, but insane at the time of the shooting. Extreme provocation—meaning the unwritten law—was a second line of defense. Thaw, according to his counsel, had been dominated by an insane impulse and compulsion, and had suffered under the delusion that he was an agent of providence.

A phalanx of medical men were brought in to support the insanity plea. One psychiatrist, Dr. Britton Evans, testified that Thaw had said to him, "I never wanted to shoot that man. I never wanted to kill him . . . Providence took charge of the situation."

Allowed in as evidence of what had contributed to Thaw's state of mind was Evelyn's account of the details she gave him—on a trip to Europe during which Thaw asked her to marry him—concerning Stanford White having drugged her in order to accomplish her seduction.

This version of Evelyn's fall had doubt cast on it by the prosecution. Under cross-examination Evelyn agreed that she had felt no bitterness against White, and had continued to see much of him after the alleged assault. But she sturdily denied having signed an affidavit which was brought before the court by White's lawyer, the notorious Abe Hummel. This document alleged that Thaw had stripped and beaten her in his efforts to induce her to sign a complaint against White, that Evelyn had resisted Thaw's coercion, maintaining that the accusations against White were false.

Evelyn, in court, admitted having gone with White to Hummel's office, but denied she had made the affidavit.

The jury, after being out for two whole days, failed to bring in a verdict. Seven had voted for murder in the first degree, five for guilty but insane.

Was Harry Thaw mad or sane? A score of psychiatrists could not agree. All mental states are in-between something or other, and here there is another in-between theory which can be considered.

On July 15—three weeks after Thaw's arrest, and months before the trial—a séance was held at Dr. Carl Wickland's home in Chicago. A doctor of medicine, and a member of the American Association for the Advancement of Science, Wickland devoted many years to the investigation of abnormal mental states. He became particularly interested in the theory of obsession by discarnate entities when he discovered, in the person of his own wife, a remarkable medium.

At this July séance, Mrs. Wickland was controlled by a spirit who said his name was Johnson. "I killed Stanford White," he declared, and gave his reason. "He deserved death. He had trifled too long with our daughters."

A man from lower down the social scale, judging by his words and manner, Johnson was fierce in denunciation of society philanderers. "They steal our children from us and put fine clothes on them, and the parents do not know what becomes of them."

Dr. Wickland asked him whether he knew he was dead. He laughed at the idea. "How could a dead person talk? The doctor said I had consumption and would die soon, but I didn't die. I never felt better in my life."

Wickland, as is the most effective procedure in such situations, advised him to examine his hands, his feet, and the clothes he was wearing. How, if he were alive, did he come to inhabit the body of a woman? After an argument Johnson was convinced the explanation was that he had died.

The next communicator made no bones about being dead. He claimed to be the father of Harry Thaw, and upheld his son's innocence.

"He is sensitive to spirit influence," he said, "and has been all his life. He was always erratic and so excitable that we were afraid to correct him for fear he would become insane. But I see our mistake now."

While he was alive he had not understood the cause of Harry's queer actions. Since his death he had realized that Harry, for most of his life, had been a tool in the hands of earthbound spirits.

"He was obsessed by revengeful spirits when he killed Stanford White."

The speaker begged Carl Wickland to write to his attorney, Mr. Olcott. The name of Olcott, the family lawyer, was unknown to Wickland at the time. He was engaged on the case, but later withdrew.

Before the séance was ended a third entity with an interest in the Thaw case controlled the medium. Like the first communicator he denounced upper-class playboys, also foolish young girls. "The rich take our girls to their dens. They put them on the stage, and the girls disown their parents."

Apart from the small detail of the lawyer's name, there is no factual evidence in all this. The profligacy of Stanford White and Harry Thaw was no secret. If the medium, Mrs. Wickland, was hardly the person to be interested, she could have picked up gossip about them quite unwittingly. The story emerging at the séance is suggestive only to this extent: fathers of betrayed maidens might well have used such phraseology in those days, though it jars on modern ears as turning pathos into bathos; and holding such sentiments, might relish as poetic justice the power to influence one philanderer to shoot another of the same ilk.

The history of abnormality, alleged by the control who claimed to be Thaw's father, found some support in the evidence given at the second trial, a year after the first. Now the defense was straight insanity. The lawyers were ready to admit mental illness on both sides of Thaw's family. A London doctor was brought over to testify to having been called to attend Thaw at Claridge's, when he found him talking disjointedly. A doctor from Paris gave evidence of an attempt at suicide. Thaw's mother said she had seen Harry weeping over the wrong done to Evelyn by White.

For the prosecution, District Attorney Jerome drew the admission from Evelyn that Thaw had known from the time of their first meeting that she was the mistress of Stanford White.

An unpredictable jury gave the verdict the defense had striven for at the first trial and, failing, had not dared ask for a second time, "Not guilty, on the ground of his insanity at the time of the commission of the act."

Lawyers and family hoped that this would mean his release, but the judge ordered that Thaw be detained in the Mattewan State Hospital for the Criminally Insane. After a series of appeals for him to be set free had been fought and lost, Thaw eventually escaped to Canada. He lost the legal struggle to remain, and was extradited to New Hampshire. There the authorities found him sane, but returned him to New York to face a charge of conspiring to defeat the ends of justice. Gaining a dismissal of the criminal charge, Thaw then appealed to the New York Supreme Court for a declaration of his sanity. He was successful. After nine years he had won his fight.

At the sanity hearings the prosecution produced new evidence to throw additional light on Thaw's abnormality, making more credible the earlier allegation that he had beaten Evelyn to force her to complain of White's conduct. A bundle of morphia needles and some whips were produced by one of his former counsel, with the statement that Thaw had given them into his keeping. A New York brothel-keeper, Susan Merrill—the defense had seen to it that she was visiting faraway places while the criminal trials were being held—now testified that Thaw had rented rooms from her to which young girls were lured by promises of stage training. She had heard screams, and had seen girls covered with welts from his beatings. Once she had rushed into the room to intervene and—so she described it—Thaw's eyes were protruding and he looked mad.

Hearing Susan Merrill's evidence in court, Evelyn Nesbit screamed out that her husband was a degenerate scoundrel for whom she had sacrificed herself and her reputation. From there on Evelyn switched sides, pleading with the judge not to release him, alleging that he had threatened to kill her.

At the final hearing Thaw was asked why he had waited four years, after he knew about Evelyn having been ruined, to shoot Stanford White.

"There is no answer to that question; I cannot give you one," was all he could say. "There was no reason."

While much of the evidence at the trials fits in with the claims made long before at the Wickland séance, only two conclusions can be clearly stated: Harry Thaw had a long-maintained enmity towards Stanford White; and he was (to whatever degree and whatever the cause) mentally unstable.

Many psychiatrists and criminologists believed that Richard Ivens, who was hanged for the murder of Bessie Hollister in Chicago, had confessed to the crime in a state of suggestion.

Dr. Hugo Munsterburg, a Harvard professor of psychology, gave the opinion that it was "an interesting and yet rather clear case of dissociation and autosuggestion." He added: "The witches of the seventeenth century were burned on account of similar confessions, and the popular understanding of mental aberrations has not made much progress since that time."

William James was as definite in diagnosing a dissociated personality. "He was not his natural self during those fateful first days, but the victim of one of those rare alterations of personality either suggested or spontaneous, which are now well known to occur in predisposed subjects."

Ivens had alternately confessed his guilt—saying that a "big man" had made him do it—and wildly denied the crime. Several months after his execution, an entity claiming to be Richard Ivens controlled the medium at a Wickland séance, and gave an explanation of the riddle.

"When I saw the woman that night I also saw the big man," he said. "My head began to feel very strange. I was grabbed by the throat and lost consciousness. When I came to myself again the big man said I had killed the woman. I had known the man for about a month, but I did not know he was a spirit. He has been hounding me ever since . . . nobody would believe me when I told them about the big fellow standing over me with a knife. He made me plead guilty. If I committed the crime I am sorry for it, but I don't know that I have done it. Why did they kill me?"

Months later one who purported to be the "big man" manifested at Wickland's circle. "I killed the woman," he declared, "but I made him confess to save my own neck." In his lifetime, he said, he had perpetrated many atrocities on women.

By psychical research standards there is nothing evidential in this account. The straightforward spirit hypothesis becomes persuasive as an explanation of puzzling factors in the Kuerten,

Thaw and Ivens cases, only when they are considered in relation to dozens of other cases, not necessarily involving criminal acts, for which there is stronger evidence of spirit interference. Again from the investigative viewpoint, tests may be more satisfactorily arranged when the subject is neither inaccessibly in jail nor has been executed.

Spirit guides claim that death is so simple and natural a process that many people do not at first realize the change. Such earthbound spirits may be attracted by the "magnetic auras" of the living and, either ignorantly or maliciously, cause mischief and misery. They can induce invalidism, immorality, crime and what appears to be insanity. This risk of obsession is the greatest pitfall facing the unwary novice in psychical research. To acknowledge this is not an argument against psychic practices or séance experiments under proper guidance. For, they warn, to be unaware of such dangers carries still greater risk for anyone, especially the susceptible neurotic. In fact, knowledge is an armor.

The spirits advise, as a means of cure, that the obsessing entity can be drawn away from the victim and attracted to a psychic intermediary—that is, a medium. After this transfer of psychoses, as it were, the troublesome spirits can more easily be reached by advanced spirits willing to help them, and the victim is relieved.

Dr. Carl Wickland became interested in testing such claims. If the validity of the hypothesis could be demonstrated, he felt it would have great bearing on much that was baffling in criminology and psychopathology.

Here we need to consider briefly some of the symptoms psychiatrists encounter in dealing with abnormal mental states. The afflicted may claim to hear voices praising, accusing or threatening them. These voices may order them to do certain things. Many will resist their delusions, but others act. In extreme instances they commit assault, suicide or murder.

Some patients show dislike or hatred of those they have loved. Or allege that their relatives or friends are being impersonated by other people.

Individuals suffer from loss of memory, fall into stupor and dream states. In some instances speech and writing will noticeably change, often with jumbled or kaleidoscopic effects. Some complain that they have lost control of their minds, and that thoughts are put into their heads by outside influences.

Now these are exactly the symptoms one would expect if the theory of spirit obsession were true. We find similar effects in cases of embryonic mediumship. And when a person without knowledge or experience sits alone for psychic development—most frequently with planchette or ouija board—the results can sometimes be frightening.

Of course, psychiatrists favor different explanations for the symptoms found in schizophrenic conditions. However, it would seem that when patients insist that outside influences press thoughts upon them, sometimes it is the simple truth. In order to distinguish obsession, efforts are needed to establish whether or not there is separate identity.

When Carl Wickland began to experiment he found—as others had done—supporting evidence for the spirit statement that the dead do not always know they are dead. At times his experiences were amusing. The owners of bodies he had been dissecting earlier in the day would turn up at the evening séance to complain. Wickland would answer, "If I were now cutting up your body at the college that would not kill you; since you yourself are here." Then he pointed out the differences between the medium's body they were controlling and their own lost carcases to convince them they had died. This did not work immediately with a colored man. Invited to look at his now-white hands, he countered, "I've got whitewash on them—whitewashing is my business."

Wickland learned that a small charge of static electricity passed through the patient could dislodge a possessing spirit, shifting it over to the medium. Other circles have found this method to work. (I do not consider its use essential, having known circles where the same apparent results were obtained without electrical apparatus being used. What matters most is the quality of the medium.)

The method described employs a Wimshurst machine to generate charges of static electricity. The subject usually holds one terminal, while the other is passed over his or her head from front to rear and down the spine. Apparently a discarnate entity is much more sensitive to the mild shock received by the patient than a human being is normally.

Lord Dowding once had a good illustration of this. The famous
Air Chief Marshal who led Fighter Command during the battle
of Britain became a Spiritualist after some of his dead pilots had
proved their survival to his satisfaction at séances, and later took
great interest in the work of "rescue" circles for the treatment of
obsession. He once asked a spirit who had experienced the
electric shock method of removal not to return to the patient
again, and got the reply, "What? Into that fire! Not likely!"

This sensitivity of discarnate entities to pain or discomfort experienced through the physical body of the subject they control
has been noted by Wickland, Dowding and many others. (I have
known trance controls of mediums to be quite fussy about their
comfort, asking for the heating in the room to be increased or
lowered, even putting on an extra woolen cardigan or taking one
off.)

This peculiarity of spirits might in a measure explain the successes of E.C.T. (electro-convulsion therapy). The severe shocks
administered, throwing the patient into convulsions, should certainly have a clearing effect if discarnate obsession is a factor in
the condition. Teeth-pulling, removal of tonsils and other infected
organs, continuous drenching with water—are among the painful
procedures which at different times have been hailed by some
doctors as effective cures for insanity. Any of them could be relied
on to dislodge the least sensitive spirit entity and send him howl-
ing into the void.

The curative effects of E.C.T. are seldom lasting. As I have
already intimated, many persons subjected to obsession, especially those leading lonely lives, come almost to love their chains.
They will unconsciously cling to, or desire renewal of, such association. Recurrence is obviously more likely if the spirits who
obsessed them to begin with have not themselves been contacted
and "rescued," but are free to return.

On the theory that earthbound spirits are attracted by the
human aura, most obsessions would seem to be largely accidental.
Once mediumistic contact has been made and the position explained to them the spirits are usually willing to leave. Even
those who retain strong material desires can be persuaded to leave
quietly when made to understand that they are doing harm to
their hosts. In some cases—which might be regarded as "multiple

personality"—a number of obsessing spirits may be involved with one subject. The demon's answer to Jesus was, "My name is Legion."

What evidence is there for the separate identity of subject and spirit? One test to establish whether the control has a distinctive individuality is by using a galvanometer to assess the emotional reactions of the medium in her normal state, then of the alleged trance control, to a series of questions. In experiments conducted at Johns Hopkins University the guides of Eileen Garrett, by the reactions they exhibited different from hers, demonstrated their independence of the medium. Catholic authorities also consider that word association tests can help to determine whether an alleged control is really a separate entity.

The same tests are applied when states of possession are suspected. If the alleged interferer reacts to ideas or associates words similarly to the subject, then his separate existence becomes doubtful.

Again, if the control speaks languages not known to the medium, it is matter for thought. Her husband claimed that Mrs. Wickland, who knew only two languages, English and Swedish, spoke six while in trance. Father Tonquedec, a Catholic well versed in the paranormal, declares that detailed replies in a foreign language will not appear to be the workings of telepathy, which is "symbolic, dim and general." Of course, he is right.

On the vexed question of secondary personalities, Carl Wickland agreed that his wife might conceivably have several. But, he argued, she could not have had the thousand personalities he had seen her exhibit. Anyone who has seen a good trance medium assume multiple guises will find it difficult to believe her to be so versatile an actress. Those who maintain it is possible have still to explain how the "secondary personalities" come to imitate recognizable characteristics and speech mannerisms of complete strangers, and give information they, and sometimes only they, would know.

Wickland amassed the best of his evidence from cases which followed the pattern: first, a definite psychosis was diagnosed in the patient; then the psychosis was transferred to the medium— that is, she manifested the characteristic symptoms of the patient's "secondary personality," which she had no normal means of know-

ing; and, finally, the psychosis was disposed of and the identity
of the obsessing spirit established. Such cases at least offer prima
facie evidence for spirit interference.

I hope no encouragement will be read into this for throwing
psychiatry out of the window. Its practitioners have won a long
and tedious battle, and good luck to them! For most of its history
medicine looked only outwards in seeking the causes of disease.
The demon theory had a long run, without heavy competition,
until the germ theory came along. Today the pendulum of opinion has swung far in favor of the involvement of the whole personality in disease. Even conservative professors of clinical
medicine are willing to range as high as ninety percent in guessing
the proportion of illnesses which are of psychosomatic origin.

After this bow to psychiatry it needs to be underlined that
there is a great deal its practitioners cannot do to cure the mentally ill patient. Schizophrenia, the term now used to describe
what was once called dementia praecox, presents a mixture of im-
pairment and preservation of mental attributes. In severe, long-
standing cases the prognosis is usually hopeless, despite the
advances claimed for drug therapy. Up to a few years ago prefrontal leucotomy was recommended when all else failed. Now it
is totally discredited. The great majority of sufferers, psychiatrists believe, are hereditarily predisposed. There is no need to
quarrel with this, or to make exaggerated claims that schizoid
states develop mainly as a result of spirit interference, in order
to suggest that obsession could be regarded as a possible factor.

The person with an inherent weakness, and that is the background of the schizophrenic, is the person most likely to be open
to an obsessing influence.

Most institutions have inmates who have been confined for
many years suffering with chronic hallucinatory psychoses. There
is no effective treatment. Eventually most sufferers become de-
mented. In this state of affairs almost anything should be worth a
trial.

Lord Dowding estimated that ten percent of people confined
in mental institutions have nothing wrong with their minds or
their brains, but are simply possessed by alien entities. This may
be a simplification. My own guess is that the possessed or obsessed are in most cases, if not all, people of a psychopathic con-

stitution to whom ignorant or evil spirits were attracted because they were more amenable, or at any rate less resistant, to attempts at interference. This may seem to be splitting hairs in an area where norms are not established. The distinction has to be emphasized because if it is looked for in isolation as the origin of any psychosis, obsession may be overlooked or wrongly dismissed when other causative factors are shown to be present.

Almost twenty years ago Lord Dowding said: "Possibly the time has scarcely arrived when this process should be pressed upon the attention of alienists, psychiatrists and the medical profession as a whole, for it is not only necessary to accept as a fact the separate existence of these discarnate spirits who are the cause of the trouble, but it is also necessary to recognize the existence of and the conscious cooperation of agents of the principle of light in the never-ending fight against darkness."

This seems to me an unnecessary acceptance of stalemate, like saying that it is no use inviting people to study the Bible unless they first become Christians. Initial belief in agents of light might well be desirable, from a practical as well as from Lord Dowding's standpoint, but it is by no means essential. What is needed on the part of psychiatrists is open-mindedness and a readiness to inquire.

Medical fashions change, methods of treatment go out of style, as has prefrontal leucotomy. William James forecast as "an absolute certainty," that the demon theory would have its run again. "One has to be scientific indeed," he added, "to be blind and ignorant enough to suspect no such possibility."

If the famous psychologist proves a true prophet it is to be hoped that the next time this theory will not be allowed to run amok. Demons do not deserve the credit for all our ills that the learnedly superstitious used to grant them.

Criminals from the psychic world do at times, however, justify a place on the list of suspects.

☐

CHAPTER EIGHT

A Witch in Time Stops Crime

PREVENTION is better than crime. But from the investigator's angle it raises a problem: the problem of proof. Claims in plenty are made for psychic warnings which may have led the receiver to avoid becoming a victim. But if due to such contrivance nothing happens, the difficulty is to be certain that without it something would.

Algernon Blackwood told me of an occasion when the Moody half of the celebrated evangelical partnership, Moody and Sankey, had his life saved by an inexplicable warning.

Moody was walking down a street in Liverpool, late at night, when suddenly he had an uncontrollable urge to cross to the other side. He had no reason at all to do so, yet he quickly darted across, puzzled by his own irrational behavior.

What would have happened had he failed to act on the impulse?

Long afterwards, a new convert at one of Moody's revivalist meetings, came forward to tell how he had been saved.

At one time, his story went, he had been a rabid opponent of Moody's brand of religion. He had gone so far as to develop a personal hatred for Moody that did not stop short of murder.

One night, in Liverpool, he had followed the evangelist along the dark streets, intending to stab him with a knife. He was behind him, his upraised arm prepared to strike, when of a sudden Moody, without turning round or giving any indication of suspicion, suddenly dashed to the other side of the street.

Moody told Blackwood this story himself. Sir Arthur Blackwood, Algernon's father, was a close friend of the evangelist, and he often visited their home when Blackwood was a boy.

Even in those days Algernon Blackwood was interested in the supernormal, and went on ghost hunts with his father. He had a varied and adventurous life before he became a writer. At séances he was urged to write by Indian guides who predicted his success. Years afterward the compulsion to write stories came upon him so strongly that he dropped all other interests, and sat at home typing, at first without any thought of publication. Many thought him to be the finest short-story writer of his day—and he certainly wrote the best ghost stories; though he admitted to me that he had never seen a ghost. But he had respect for his Indian guides; which was not surprising after the ability they had shown as talent spotters.

Moody's experience can be interpreted in more ways than one. A subconscious or hyperaesthetic sensing of danger does seem less likely than the explanation that he received a psychic prod from outside, remembering that he felt no fear, only bewilderment, at his conduct. Unlike the chicken, he didn't know why he crossed the road!

Much more satisfactory than the warning which forestalls events is direct intervention which exposes a crime already in commission. Robert Lynd, whom I regarded as the last of the great essayists in the tradition of Lamb, Steele and Hazlitt, told me a story which offers a good example. I cannot give the name of the woman involved but in addition to being a friend of Robert Lynd she had been taken to the séance in question by Sir Oliver Lodge, so her integrity is well vouched for.

At the séance her dead husband purported to communicate, and revealed to her that she was being robbed by the manager of the brickworks owned by the family. She had not gone to the séance for that sort of information, and had no suspicion of the kind herself.

When she returned home she called in the manager, and asked him to show her the books. Looking through the books she found them, as Lynd put it, "a bit shaky."

She accused the manager of defrauding her.

"How did you get on to it?" he asked.

"I heard about it from my husband's ghost," she said. At that the man went white, and confessed everything.

There are dangers and a ridiculous side to seemingly psychic warnings, as a personal story of Robert Lynd's well illustrates. He and some friends—one of them Naomi Mitchison, the writer —who were staying in the same hotel were experimenting with a planchette.

To their consternation they got a warning that there would be poisoned cabbage served in the dinner next night.

"We didn't know what to do about it," Lynd recalled wryly. "If we had warned our fellow guests we should have become very unpopular with the landlady. Fortunately, when the dinner arrived there was no cabbage—we had runner beans instead!"

Suicide is a crime in the eyes of the law, though on the whole attempts which fail are dealt with leniently nowadays. Even the judges, who are seldom in the vanguard of legal reform, have come to realize that a state of mind which induces self-murder is punishment enough in itself; and, except where the act is attempted as a means of escaping retribution for other crimes, is much more a medical than a legal problem. Indeed, one might reflect that while individual freedom of decision has contracted in many ways, man's right to dispose of himself is more widely recognized as a matter between him and his Creator—or, alternatively, his psychiatrist. But to help an imminent suicide stay alive remains, technically, prevention of crime. Even when the lifesaver is an outlaw witch.

Early in World War II, Estelle Roberts was demonstrating clairvoyance to 2500 people at the Queen's Hall, the famous London concert house which soon after became an air raid casualty. At this time—and up to 1951—mediums were classed as witches under English law.

In the midst of delivering a message to a person in the audience, Estelle suddenly stopped, and pointed to a man in the balcony.

"Give me your word," she said, "that you will come and see me after the meeting."

He nodded dumbly. Estelle Roberts carried on smoothly from where she broke off.

When the meeting was over the man went round backstage as he had promised.

"Now," the medium commanded, "give me the poison you have in your pocket."

The man countered, "I don't know what you're talking about."

"Either give it to me or I will take it."

The man hesitated. There were officials and journalists standing close by. Then, seeing how determined she was, he drew from his pocket a paper packet and handed it over.

"Now you have that you might as well have the other thing," he forestalled her by saying. "Here you are—here is the razor!"

Then he broke down, head in hands. When he had recovered he told his tragic story. His wife had died after a painful illness. He had lost his job. With no hope and no one to hold on to he had exhausted his courage, and decided to put an end to everything.

Early that evening he had been sitting on a bench in Hyde Park, waiting for the fall of darkness to cover his act. A sheet of paper, blown by the wind, flattened itself out against his feet. He glanced down, and saw staring up at him the bold words: *YOU CANNOT DIE!* And below this: *Estelle Roberts at the Queen's Hall.*

He bent and picked up the paper. It was a flyer announcing the meeting to be held that night. The words, so apposite to his intentions, struck him forcibly. The Queen's Hall was not very far. He thought he would go along there to pass the time before dark.

And from 2500 people crowded into the concert hall, Estelle Roberts picked out the one man whose life it was urgent to save.

I have known a great many mediums, but can think of no other who would have been so nerveless and so sure in handling a situation of this kind. However, the episode, apart from the dramatic impact, is not unique.

Mrs. James Wilson was crossing William Street in the city of Perth, western Australia, when a woman grasped her arm. She may have recognized Mrs. Wilson as a well-known local Spiritualist, for in great distress she began to pour out a story of evil spirits haunting her home.

They were halted in the middle of the roadway. Mrs. Wilson

guided the distraught woman on to the sidewalk. When they were safe from the traffic, she said, "There is no need to tell me what you were going to tell me; I already know."

"What do you know?" the woman asked nervously.

"That you were going to jump under a tram."

The woman was startled. "How could you know that?"

Mrs. Wilson smiled. "Your dead mother is standing behind you at this moment, and she is telling me." She went on reassuringly, "There are no evil spirits in your home. Go back there, pick up the note you left on the table for your children—and destroy it."

"You know all about it," the woman said, incredulously.

"I do," Mrs. Wilson nodded.

"But you don't know what I wrote in the letter?"

"You asked your children to go to the morgue at the Perth Hospital to identify your body."

The woman burst into tears. Mrs. Wilson took her firmly by the arm.

"Go home; and as you turn the key in your door, call on the Lord Jesus Christ to be with you."

The would-be suicide did as she had advised, Mrs. Wilson learned afterwards when, during a meeting at the Perth Town Hall, she came and thanked her for saving her life. Since that day, she said, she had been troubled by evil spirits, real or fanciful, no longer.

Even the lay person may become an instrument of psychic intervention on occasion. Mrs. H. H. Rushford, deputy chairman of the Durham magistrates and the city of Durham's first woman mayor, had such an experience.

The story began when a young student and church organist, wanting money to buy presents for his girl friend, forged his brother's name to a check. Although it was his first offense the circumstances were felt to warrant a jail sentence.

He was only one of thousands who had appeared before Mrs. Rushford during her eighteen years on the bench.

The morning came when the young man was due for release. Mrs. Rushford woke early with an uneasy feeling she could not shake off. She knew she must go to the railway station where the boy would be catching the train to his home.

She found him standing apart from the other travelers waiting on the platform. He recognized her immediately.

Mrs. Rushford asked him if he would like to have a cup of tea with her before taking the train. In the station buffet, his tension relaxing as they talked, he confessed to her that, unable to face his people at home, he had intended to throw himself under the engine.

By talking over his problems she was able to bring him to a different frame of mind. And coincidentally, or so one imagines, a friend of hers who was an organist happened to be at the station. It was just the company the boy needed, and Mrs. Rushford was able to arrange for them to travel together.

It puzzles many Spiritualists that they can go on being fervent believers in spirit guidance for years without receiving direct advice on their problems, while strangers to Spiritualistic ideas often get aid seemingly out of the blue. I have listened to innumerable complaints, wry or bewildered, on this theme.

If I was asked to pick someone to argue the Spiritualist case for survival, cogently and without demagoguery or high-flown fancy, I would probably name Horace Leaf. In fact, when organizers of platform debates and radio discussions appealed to me I usually advised them to get in touch with him. Besides being a well-known lecturer in England, Leaf made many trips abroad. In 1936 he was acting on behalf of the executive council of the American Society for Psychical Research, in an investigation of Frank Decker's mediumship.

On the way from New York to Boston, where they were going for a series of test séances, Leaf and Decker stopped off in Connecticut at the home of a Mr. Jonson. (This is not his real name, which in this instance cannot be given.)

Although Decker was received with an enthusiasm which, as Leaf put it, would have flattered royalty, it soon became obvious that the Jonson family knew very little about Spiritualism or psychic matters generally. Jonson was plainly a man of wealth and intelligence. Whatever it was that had given him such a profound respect for Decker's talents, Leaf surmised, must have been out of the ordinary. Late that evening, alone with his host for the first time, he angled the conversation in a way he hoped would bring an explanation.

"What! Has Mr. Decker not told you?" Jonson was greatly surprised. "Why, sir, that man saved the fortune of my family, and through his powers rendered me a most remarkable service."

Jonson's story went back a few years to the time when he made a business trip to Russia on behalf of a large corporation. He was operating on a percentage basis, and the enterprise turned out to be remarkably successful. On his return to the States the corporation owed him upwards of fifty thousand dollars.

He soon learned that the firm intended to double-cross him. For months he went on negotiating with corporation executives, but they refused to pay their debt. Jonson was scared of taking them to court. He knew they had a lot of political pull, and unreasonably or not, believed he would not get a square deal.

A final meeting was arranged. Jonson made up his mind the night before that he would have to settle for his expenses, amounting to only three thousand dollars. He told no one of his decision, which he was most unhappy about.

Hoping it would improve his frame of mind he went for a walk. On the street he met a man he knew, stopped to talk, and was invited by his friend to go to a direct voice séance.

Jonson was both uninformed and uninterested in what that might be. His friend's explanation left him with the idea that it was some kind of vaudeville show. He thought it might cheer him up, or at least take his mind off his worries, so he went along.

About twenty people were gathered in the room when they arrived. Soon the lights were lowered, and then voices began to speak. Jonson found the whole business very confusing. He scarcely realized that the conversations he was hearing were with people supposedly dead.

When he heard someone address him by his own name he was startled. The speaker introduced himself as Riley. Jonson had never known anyone of that name so far as he could recall; least of all a farmer, which was what the man claimed to have been. Farmer Riley seemed to know all about him, however, for he came straight to the point.

"Mr. Jonson, these people owe you fifty-four thousand dollars —and we are going to see that they pay you!"

Jonson was shocked beyond belief. His amazement did not

lessen when the voice made it clear that his current thinking was known.

"You shall not settle for your out-of-pocket expenses," Farmer Riley said. "Will you make me a promise, Mr. Jonson?"

Jonson was so bewildered he gave the promise without stopping to think.

"You can imagine my state of mind when I said I would do anything he requested," Jonson explained to Horace Leaf. "No intelligent man would give his word of honor until he knew what it was about. Yet I did just that."

"Good," came Riley's terse response when Jonson consented. "Now this is what I want you to do. As soon as you enter the room tomorrow, and meet the executives, start talking—and don't stop!"

This was the end of the séance so far as Jonson's affairs were concerned.

Next morning Jonson, waiting in the reception room before his interview, still felt hopeless about the matter. "I was wondering what I could say, and could think of absolutely nothing. During the nine months of negotiation I had laid all my cards on the table. I had none left to play.

"But the moment I entered the boardroom I started talking. To my own amazement I began making a series of charges against the corporation, criminal accusations that I would have expected to get me a ten-year sentence for libel."

The effect on the men round the table was even more astonishing. The secretary of the corporation turned as white as a sheet. He leaned towards the chairman and said, "By God, he has the dope on us."

"I came out of the room with this check in my hand. . . ." Taking the check from his wallet Jonson showed it to Leaf. "That is a certified check for eighteen thousand dollars," he said, "and as good as solid cash. I keep it about me to show my friends —and to assure myself I am not dreaming. The next day I received the balance of what was owing to me."

I have known many instances—none of them involving fifty-four thousand dollars, I should add—of the unbeliever being helped, and the faithful allotted the role of Job. If you like, you can interpret Mr. Jonson's experience as indicating that the spirit world is not above putting on the pressure by way of a little ungentle blackmail; or you may say that villainy was rewarded by a just comeuppance, and a conspiracy to defraud defeated.

Villainy was meted out its just deserts in another story which reveals the spirit world as possessing a perhaps unsuspected capacity for devious intrigue.

This account I had from Dr. P. Yotopoulos, Professor of Penal Law at the University of Athens, just a few years ago. The events took place when the distinguished Greek lawyer was a young man, studying for his doctorate in Rome, about the turn of the century. The period is important, for the climax of the tale is a Ruritanian romp of psychic world dimensions.

Yotopoulos was living in the Via Dei Pastini, near the Pantheon, where he became acquainted with another student, Roberto Lombardo, who had a room on the same floor. Lombardo, in his last year at the University, was studying philology.

They formed the habit of taking a walk together in the afternoons, and one day, when the weather was too bad to go out of doors, Lombardo suggested they might attempt some psychic experiments to pass the time.

Yotopoulos was shocked at the idea. "How can you believe in such things?" he demanded.

"I don't," Lombardo protested, "but there is something strange that is worth investigating."

Yotopoulos had the feeling that Lombardo was more of a believer than he pretended, but nevertheless did not refuse to try the experiment.

They placed their fingers lightly on a small, three-legged table. Astoundingly, messages came—and to the consternation of Yotopoulos they revealed knowledge of a love affair he had had in Paris. Lombardo could not have known about it, and he himself would not have willed such a disclosure.

Had they contacted playful or malicious spirits? Yotopoulos was mildly alarmed when the session closed with the message, "I shall come to visit you tonight."

There was an extra bed in his room. Wanting company he invited Lombardo to stay and see what would happen.

They had been lying on their beds for only a few minutes, with a candle still burning, when pillows were pulled from under both their heads simultaneously and thrown to the floor.

They had barely recovered from this when a walking stick hanging on a hook was thrown to the ground. Next the circular metal lid of a receptacle fell off, and began to roll in circles on the floor.

After it stopped rolling Yotopoulos picked it up and put it outside the door, which he then locked. The lid was returned to the room, through the locked door, it would seem, and continued to rotate.

Further telekinetic phenomena insured that the two students spent a troubled and sleepless night.

The following evening they went to the theater, then sat out late at a café, unwilling to go home to a repetition of the disturbance. While they were there a friend came by, and asked what kept them out at that hour. He was Alfredo Cortini, a third-year medical student.

Hearing the reason for their reluctance to go home, despite being tired from not having slept the night before, Cortini was amused. He would go along to protect them, he said with a chuckle.

The trio went to Yotopoulos' room. Cortini entered first, calling out, "Where are you, my dear spirits? Let me admire you, too."

No sooner had he finished speaking than the drawer of a dresser burst open. One after the other, the water sketches inside it tumbled out. Then books stacked on a table cascaded to the floor.

Cortini's boldness deserted him. He said he had to go home as his people were expecting him, and departed forthwith. Yotopoulos and Lombardo passed through another hectic night of phenomena.

In the morning Cortini was back to visit them. During the night, things had happened in the room where he slept with his brother, including noisy movements from a bicycle which stood firmly on a metal rack.

Lombardo's idea was to hold a séance so that they could be given help to get rid of the boisterous influences. They tried this, and were advised that the three of them should hold regular sittings.

The spirit making this suggestion, they were informed, was a great-uncle of Yotopoulos named Spiridon.

If it was his great-uncle, Yotopoulos had a question. "Is it true," he asked, "that you committed an injustice against my father?"

"Yes, unfortunately," was the answer.

"And did you win the lawsuit through a false oath?"

"I swore falsely on the urn containing the relics of St. Spiridon."

This seemed to Yotopoulos to be partly true and partly in error. He knew that his father had once taken legal action against his great-uncle, and that the judge had exacted an oath from Spiridon. But he thought the communicator must be mistaken in saying that Spiridon had sworn on the urn of the saint—his namesake—rather than on the Bible.

Yet to his great surprise his father, when he wrote to ask, confirmed that that was how it was. When Yotopoulos then checked for himself the law statutes applying at the time he discovered that Article 41 laid down, as he had expected, that "The oath is given on the Holy Bible in the presence of the judge and the public priest."

However, the next article stated that if the judge thought it necessary "the oath might be taken in a church where there is a holy corpse, or an ikon of especial sacredness. Present at the oath-taking should be the secretary or assistant secretary of the court, and the public priest or another priest."

In the index of the *Leggi Municipali* he found a statement that there had been a custom of taking oaths on the urn of St. Spiridon.

This obscure and outdated Greek practice, unfamiliar to Yotopoulos who had just completed the thesis for his doctorate in law, was hardly likely to be known to either of his friends, Italians whose subjects were medicine and philology.

While this evidence strengthened his confidence in the communications, Yotopoulos would have been badly shaken could he have anticipated the drama into which he and his two companions were to be flung.

The first intimation they had, though its relevance was not at the time apparent, came with the advice that Lombardo ought to continue his fencing lessons, which he had stopped taking, because the skill would prove to be useful.

At another séance Yotopoulos was reminded about his twenty-year-old cousin, who was living with her mother and brother in Paris. There was a man she had known in Athens, whose attentions she had rejected . . . this much Yotopoulos already knew.

Then came the revelation. The man intended to pursue her. Even worse, he schemed to abduct her, and had bribed the family servant, and through him the concierge at the Paris apartment, to admit him at a time when both mother and brother would be absent. In order to secure his admission he was going to pose as a priest from Athens.

Abduction, if not common, was not a lapsed sport among the Greeks in those good old days. More fantastic than the plot was the spirit counterplot to foil it.

First, Yotopoulos was instructed to ask his father for a sum equivalent to twenty pounds, a much larger amount than it strikes us today. It would be required for expenses. When the money came the three young men were told to make ready for a trip.

The would-be abductor, they were advised, planned to travel to Paris by way of Italy. Yotopoulos and Lombardo were ordered to Bologna to intercept him. Cortini's mission was to go to Barre. Then came the somewhat unnerving outline of what would happen:

"After four days Lombardo will have a duel. He will be wounded first, but continuing the fight, will wound his adversary seriously though not mortally, with the stroke he was taught in the lesson this morning." The reason why Lombardo had been recommended to keep on with his lessons was now clear. The stroke referred to consisted of two feints at the right shoulder, followed by a real thrust at the left breast.

The day after their arrival in Bologna, Yotopoulos and Lombardo received more instructions through the table. Lombardo was to go alone—Yotopoulos was known to the man from Athens and would be recognized—to a certain café. He would see the man there, dressed as a priest. He was to sit at a table near him, and find some means to offer him insult. The mock priest would get angry, and it would end in a challenge to a duel.

It came about exactly as the communicator had foretold. Lombardo found his man at the café, and began to make fun of his attire. After enduring the insults for a time, the "priest" burst out angrily, "You laugh, but I am able to make you cry." And then threw out a challenge.

The proprieties of the dueling code were observed. The disputants appointed seconds, Lombardo had choice of weapons, and the meeting was arranged.

The fight took place at a remote spot in the country outside Bologna on June 1, 1899. Two physicians were present with first aid materials; two cabs stood by prepared to rush one or both of the contestants to a private hospital if the necessity arose. The duelists faced each other, touched swords. After only a few passes Lombardo's opponent pinked him in the left arm. Ordinarily, this would have been enough to satisfy honor in such a bout. To the surprise of his adversary—and also of the witnesses who knew of no serious cause for enmity between the two men—Lombardo insisted, as soon as he had been bandaged, that the fight should continue.

They again took up their swords. This time, after a few rallies, Lombardo wounded his opponent in the left shoulder, by the stroke he had been taught on a certain morning.

All had happened as the spirit messages predicted.

When the doctors had tended the loser, Lombardo sought to speak to him privately. The man asked, "Why do you trouble me?"

"Because you are a criminal," Lombardo answered, speaking as he had been instructed. "You poisoned your wife in Athens in such a manner that her death has been attributed to natural causes."

The other blanched. "How do you know about this?"

"It was told to me and Yotopoulos by a spirit who was his relative. If you have escaped human justice you cannot escape divine wrath. But as if one crime were not sufficient you were preparing to commit a new one." And Lombardo told his startled victim exactly what his plans were in going to Paris.

If this were not enough to daunt the stoutest criminal, Cortini's role in Barre had yet to be played.

Cortini, after his arrival there, had the impulse to do automatic writing one night, and in this way received his instructions.

He was to go next day to meet an express train which would be stopping for a quarter of an hour at the central station. In a special sleeping car he would find a wounded man . . . the man about whom much information had been given at the séances in Rome. Cortini was to say to him, "You are a criminal . . ." the rest of the script following almost word for word the message Lombardo had been given to say.

Cortini met the train, and delivered the warning to a much perturbed Lothario. Evidently it put an end to the evildoer's designs. His machinations doubly exposed, he lost heart and returned to Athens.

The trio of students received a final message from Yotopoulos' uncle. "Now, after all you have seen, your responsibility for all immoral deeds is greater." And his farewell advice, "Trust to holy guidance and your conscience."

On such a moralizing tone the séances ended and the little circle broke up.

I confess that when Professor Yotopoulos gave me this story the Ruritanian tang made much of it difficult to swallow. The man who was to become a distinguished professor of penal law, a member of the committee which drafted new Greek legislation after the second world war, could be expected to have a sense of logic and evidence even in his younger days, which would not allow him to be duped by his friends to this extent. If anyone played tricks it was much more likely to be Yotopoulos himself. It was he who had the background information and knew the characters in the plot. It was Lombardo and Cortini who took on the dangerous roles, one to fight a duel, both to accuse a stranger to his face of crimes including murder. They were not deceivers, but wholehearted believers if they did these things.

There is the if—that Yotopoulos may have been pulling my leg, always a possibility up to the onset of rigor mortis. Elderly professors are not the likeliest perpetrators of such elaborate jokes, but in the case of Professor Yotopoulos another factor altogether makes the idea incredible. As president of the Greek Society for Psychic Studies, who in his writings and lectures has done much to encourage interest in the serious aspects of the subject, he would be about the last person to invent an escapade of his youth which could make it the target of ridicule.

When Sir Oliver Lodge published messages which made mention of whisky and cigars being enjoyed in the spirit world he was laughed at by the skeptical. He could have avoided the mockery quite simply by leaving out such references. Obviously he was aware of this, and their inclusion was seen by the discerning among his contemporaries as an example of his admired integrity. In much the same way, I incline to believe, Professor Yotopoulos described the events and attitudes displayed just as he remembers them to have been. They were nearer then, in time and in spirit, to the adventurous days of the original Three Musketeers.

As for the devious maneuvers of the spirit counterplot—well, there again, it takes all kinds to make a spirit world. And Greatuncle Spiridon was a Greek!

There are as problematic aspects in another personal story told to me by a British Home Secretary after his retirement. In this instance a ghost, if ghost it was, bypassed mediums and policemen and went to the topmost authority.

The Right Honorable J. R. Clynes was Minister for Home Affairs from 1929 to 1931. One of the most sensational murder trials during this period resulted in a man named Podmore being sentenced to death for the killing of a Southampton garage proprietor.

Shortly before the date set for execution there was a suggestion that new evidence in Podmore's favor might be forthcoming. Clynes, who was on holiday, cut it short so as to be on hand if a last-minute reprieve seemed to be justified.

On the night of his return to London—two days before the hanging was due—Clynes was sitting in his study, quietly reading, when there came a knock at the door. The rest of the household were in bed, so he went to answer it himself.

"It was a queer sort of knock," he said, in recollecting. "It sounded as if it was made with a stick or a bony hand. The time was just on midnight."

When the Home Secretary opened the door . . . "I saw in the darkness in front of me a slim figure, closely bearded, looking like an apparition from the grave."

The manifestant spoke to him in a low voice. "I have come to talk to you about the hammer used in the murder case."

Clynes was shocked both by the appearance and by the voice of his visitor. At last he gave the answer he was bound to give to any caller, that it would be improper for him to discuss such a matter in private. He invited the visitor to see him next morning at the Home Office.

"I cannot come . . . *then,*" was the strange reply.

And the figure turned, and faded into the night.

Clynes did not hear again from his ghostly visitor. No new evidence came that would have enabled him to grant a reprieve, and the condemned man was duly executed.

This incident is the more puzzling because the Podmore case cannot be ranked among the really doubtful convictions for murder.

However, there is no doubt at all that J. R. Clynes was deeply impressed by his experience, years afterward when I knew him, and not less so at the time.

For, although Podmore did not escape the gallows, Clynes became the first Home Secretary to attempt to abolish capital punishment. His government was turned out of office before the measure could pass through Parliament.

☐

CHAPTER NINE

Bury Him Not on the Lone Prairie

AN August noon in Texas. Five men riding under the burning sun pulled up their horses at a spot where the animals could graze while the men rested in the shade and ate a lunch of bully beef. Three of the men unsaddled their mounts. Two merely loosened the bridles.

The year was 1833. The place, later to be called Pecan Spring, was five miles northwest of what is now Austin, the capital city of Texas. The small party was led by one of the first settlers in the area, Josiah Wilbarger, a man from Missouri.

Wilbarger had located on the banks of the Colorado River, a few miles above the crossing of the Camino Real linking San Antonio and Nacogdoches. His nearest neighbor had been thirty miles away until his friend, Reuben Hornsby, came and built a log cabin only seven miles up river.

The Hornsby place became a kind of welcoming center for homesteaders. Hornsby, his wife Sarah, and Wilbarger did much to help newcomers find locations. The names Wilbarger's Creek and Hornsby's Bend came to commemorate these outposts of pioneer hospitality.

Wilbarger was now undertaking one of his neighborly missions. His four companions, Christian, Strother, Haynie and Standifer, were looking for headrights. They had spent the night at Hornsby's, and Wilbarger had ridden over early to guide them on a surveying trip to the northwest.

Their morning ride had been without incident except for sighting a lone Indian near Walnut Creek, watching them from a hilltop. He galloped into a cedar bluff and disappeared when Wilbarger headed towards him. Wilbarger felt a little uneasy, wondering if the brave might be scouting for a war party. But a little while later, when the others wanted to make camp, he raised no objection.

They were still at their meal when the ambush was sprung. Suddenly a fusillade of shots and arrows poured on them from every direction.

Strother fell at the first volley . . . dead. Christian was severely wounded. Wilbarger, struck in hip and calf, tried to drag Christian behind a tree, not realizing he was too far gone to survive.

Haynie and Standifer were doubly fortunate. As yet they were untouched by bullet or arrow, and they were the two who had not unsaddled their mounts. They ran for their horses as fifty or more Indians broke cover. Wilbarger dropped again, this time with an arrow in his throat.

The last Haynie and Standifer saw of him he was on the ground, surrounded by the main body of Indians, all bent on lifting his scalp. Convinced that their companions were beyond help, the two survivors spurred their mounts into a wild gallop, and managed to outrun their pursuers.

They reached the Hornsby place with their tragic story. The question in every mind was, Would the Indians attack the cabin? It was strongly built, with the added protection of a stockade, in anticipation of such danger. However, a rider sent to carry the sad tidings of Wilbarger's death to his home, was told to bring reinforcements just in case.

Around midnight Sarah Hornsby roughly shook her husband awake. "Wilbarger is not dead," she cried agitatedly. "He sits against an oak tree. He is scalped and bleeding. He is covered with blood from his wounds, but he is not dead. I have seen him plainly."

Her upraised voice carried to the men in the next room. They then heard Reuben Hornsby speak soothingly, reminding his wife what Standifer and Haynie said they had seen. A wounded man at the mercy of fifty Indians could never have survived. Eventually, Hornsby succeeded in quieting her, and they all went back to sleep.

For a few hours . . . At three o'clock Sarah aroused them again.

"I saw him again," she cried with utter conviction. "Josiah Wilbarger is alive as sure as God lives. His only covering is the blood from his wounds, but he is alive."

Heedless of her husband's protestations this time, Sarah threw on a dress, lit candles, and called in the men. Haynie and Standifer both tried to tell her that she was insisting upon the impossible. They had seen Wilbarger fall, Indians rushing to scalp him from all around. Practically speaking, he had died before their eyes.

"Maybe you were too busy running to see straight," Sarah snapped back. "I don't care what you think you saw. I have seen Wilbarger as clearly as I now see you. He is suffering tortures, waiting for help. If you are not cowards"—she swept them all with her glance—"you will go to him at once. If you fail him he will die."

Reuben Hornsby hesitated. Wilbarger was his friend, and Sarah's emphatic belief had impressed him. He compromised. They must wait for more men. He could not leave her and the children unprotected.

Sarah poured scorn on this argument. She was a frontier wife, able to cope with anything. She had seen men killed by Indians, and had helped to bury them. She had protected herself before, she reminded Reuben, showing herself dressed in men's clothes, gun in hand, to scare off marauders. If Indians came near she could take the children and lie hidden in the dogwood thicket.

The men remained unwilling to leave before dawn. So Sarah busied herself getting food ready. She gave them sheets to bury Christian and Strother in, and to make a litter for carrying Wilbarger. She thought he would be unable to sit a horse. When the extra men came, Reuben Hornsby and his friends were ready to ride.

At the camp by Pecan Spring they found the bodies of Christian and Strother, lying where they had fallen. They buried them together under a tree.

There was no sign of Wilbarger's body near the camp. The men fanned out to make a search. It was late afternoon before they found him for he had crawled a long distance after the raid.

On first sighting the naked, blood-caked form propped under a big oak tree they mistook him for an Indian, and approached with caution.

But it was indeed Wilbarger, a terrible sight with his fleshless skull, yet still breathing. Gently they wrapped him in a sheet, and lifted him up to Hornsby's saddle. Sarah had been wrong on just one point—her idea that they would need to make a litter. They rode very slowly back to the house.

There his wounds were properly dressed, and with Sarah's careful nursing he recovered, though his head never healed completely.

Long before he was up and about, Wilbarger had told a story as remarkable as Sarah Hornsby's experience.

The arrow in the throat, he said, had paralyzed him for a time. He was conscious while the scalping knife cut at his head, and hair and flesh were torn away. Yet he felt no pain, only a sensation like the clap of thunder. The Indians stripped his body, and because he lay so inert and showed no reaction must have assumed him to be dead.

The gaping hole in his neck made it unnecessary for them to cut his throat, as they had done with Christian and Strother—so the arrow hitting him there had been twice lucky.

For a long while after the scalping, Wilbarger drifted back and forth between awareness and unawareness. During his conscious periods he found he could move, but with the loss of paralysis came pain. He tried to stand and failed. The most he could do was to crawl. Fortunately, his sense of direction was not impaired. He knew where the waterhole was, and dragged himself to it to relieve his agonizing thirst.

Wilbarger lay there in the cooling water until the sun began to slip down in the western sky. Then, painfully and laboriously, he started to drag himself in the direction of the Hornsby house. At last he could go no farther. Exhausted beyond measure he propped himself against a tree.

The strangest part of his experience occurred about midnight. All at once he was no longer alone. Before him stood the figure of a woman—and, wonder of wonders, a woman he knew, his sister Margaret Clifton. But Margaret lived far away in Missouri!

He heard her saying, in a calm, comforting voice, "Brother

Josiah, you are too weak to go farther by yourself. Rest here under the tree, and before the sun sets your friends will come to care for you."

She began to move away—in the direction of the Hornsby house. Wilbarger could not question for a moment the reality of the vision. Indeed, Margaret's form was so vivid, her words so clear, that he pleaded with her to stay with him.

As near as the times could be calculated, Sarah Hornsby's first vision of Wilbarger must have come soon after he saw and heard his sister. Both Mrs. Hornsby and Wilbarger had such reputations for character and integrity that no one who knew them ever doubted their word, and they told their respective parts of this story often.

It was already a local wonder when, some months later, news came to Wilbarger of the death of his sister Margaret. Seven hundred miles away in Missouri, at her home in Florissant, near St. Louis, she had died the day before the Indians scalped Wilbarger.

Plainly read, these linked experiences suggest that after appearing to her brother the spirit of Margaret Clifton went on to the Hornsby cabin—the direction in which Wilbarger swore he had seen her moving—and there prompted the vision that saved his life.

Texas legends came in large sizes, but this is a more authentic-seeming tale than most, from there or elsewhere.

Wilbarger lived for eleven years after his scalping. He died as the result of accidentally striking his exposed skull against the timber of a cotton gin. They were tough, mighty tough, in the West!

In this incident the Indians were cast as the "baddies" with the Hornsby and Wilbarger clans representing the best type of frontier people—which they were. Although, on a broader historical view, my sympathy is mainly with the redman.

As a movement, the Spiritualists were the first, I think, to allow dignity to the redman. This was because many spirit guides claimed to be North American Indians. The guides, or the Spiritualists, explained this by saying that the Indians had practiced forms of psychic communication when on earth as part of their religion. Therefore, accepting spirit return as a natural thing, it was as natural that they should now take a prominent part at séances. Of course, anti-Spiritualists jeered at the idea that savages could teach them anything, either here or from the hereafter.

A good deal of exaggerated nonsense was talked on both sides. It became a badge of pride to many foolish Spiritualists to have an Indian directing them. Some even quarreled about rights of possession. Their opponents pretended to believe that all guides were Indians—though plenty of them claimed European nationality—and made weak jokes about their names.

Séance devotees are often prone to wishful romanticism. Living a dull life in an industrial suburb a housewife might well be titillated by the glamour of having captured the interest of a mysterious Indian—or an ancient Egyptian, for that matter. Numerically, Egyptians probably come second in the guide popularity poll.

There is a parallel in what I might term the reincarnation ploy. Many people of no importance in this life are susceptible to the flattering notion that they were persons of importance in a past life—a Pharaoh, a Greek philosopher, a priest of the temple at Jerusalem. The slaves who did the back-breaking toil in building the Pyramids, the hoplites who died under the swords of Cyrus, even the nameless five thousand who ate the loaves and the fishes, seem to have vanished from the reincarnationary cycle.

John Keats believed he had a presiding genius, and hoped it might be Will Shakespeare influencing him from the next world. The idea is not ridiculous because Keats soars amid the topmost flight of poets after Shakespeare. Evan Powell believed he was guided by Black Hawk, the famous leader of the Fox and Sauk tribes who with forty warriors defeated 270 Kentucky riflemen. Powell, whom I knew well, was one of the finest mediums of his age and a man of noble character, so again the idea is not nonsensical. But why Tecumseh, one of the greatest redmen in history, should waste his time on the round dozen people I have heard claim him as guide, most of them well loved by their mothers no doubt, but with no visible distinction of talent or character to recommend them, is beyond my comprehension.

Reincarnation could be true—but little Tutankhamens reborn in every village? Indian guides may be real—but Sitting Bull at every séance? One shudders at the thought.

Spiritualists, or spirit guides themselves, have offered an explanation which undercuts criticism of the Indians as being lacking in spiritual refinements. The more evolved spirits, they say, are too remote from earth conditions to communicate directly, and use the Indians as an intermediate link—something like a telephone relay system. Whether or not this occurs in certain instances, as an apology for the Indians it is not necessary.

What few Spiritualists, and fewer of their critics, have taken the trouble to find out, is that the claims they first made for the redman have good historical backing. The pejorative tag that the only good Injun was a dead Injun has little support, even from the frontiersmen who did battle with them.

Serious commentators, from Christopher Columbus onward, voice a continuing theme. Columbus wrote to Ferdinand and Isabella: "I swear to your Majesties that there is not a better people in the world than these; more affectionate, affable, or mild. They love their neighbors as themselves, and they always speak smilingly." The Pilgrim Fathers met with the same friendly reception. Invariably the colonists were first to deal badly with the Indians, rather than the reverse. It was Tecumseh who stopped the English army under General Proctor from torturing their prisoners during the War of Independence.

The Smithsonian authority, Garrick Mallery, wrote that the North American Indians "habitually lived in and by religion to a degree comparable with that of the old Israelites under the theocracy." George Catlin, in *Manners, Customs and Conditions of the North American Indians,* also compares their way of life with that of the Biblical Jews.

After sixty years' experience of the Choctaws in Texas, John James claimed for them "the purest religion, and the loftiest conceptions of the Great Creator," explaining that the North American Indian had no priests, no idols, no sacrifices, "but went direct to the Great Spirit and worshipped Him. . . ."

Captain Bonneville wrote of the Nez Percés and Flatheads: "Simply to call these people religious would convey but a faint idea of the deep hue of piety and devotion which pervades their whole conduct. Their honesty is immaculate, and their purity of purpose and their observance of the rites of their religion are most uniform and remarkable. They are certainly more like a nation of saints than a horde of savages."

Some of the missionaries were as complimentary. The Reverend C. Van Dusen, who knew the Ojibways, held the opinion that "the genuine North American pagan presents to the world the most noble specimen of the natural man that can be found on the face of the earth."

In almost the same words, Bishop Henry Whipple of Minnesota wrote, "The North American Indian is the noblest type of a heathen man on earth. He recognizes a Great Spirit; he believes in immortality; he has a quick intellect; he is a clear thinker; he is brave and fearless, and, until betrayed, he is true to his plighted faith. . . ."

Much of this supports the claims of the spirit communicators who claimed to have lived on earth as Indians. Talking about their psychic powers, Dr. Charles A. Eastman, himself of Sioux ancestry, says that while it is fair to assume that there were imposters, "Yet there are well-attested instances of remarkable prophecies and other mystic practice. . . . I sometimes fancy that such nearness to nature as I have described keeps the spirit sensitive to impressions not commonly felt, and in touch with unseen powers."

It would appear that crime as we know it scarcely existed among some tribes of Indians when the whites first encountered them. Lewis Henry Morgan wrote, "Crimes and offences were so infrequent, under their social system, that the Iroquois can scarcely be said to have had a criminal code."

Father Jerome Lalemant remarked of the Hurons that "we find without comparison much less disorder than there is in France, though here the mere shame of having committed the crime is the offender's punishment." Perhaps, as penologists might agree, a society gets the criminals it deserves.

Alas for the North American Indian, he could not resist the corrupting force of historical progress. Missionaries and scholars have denounced the undermining influence of white and (nominally, at least) Christian civilization. More eloquent than they, at a down to earth level, was the Hudson's Bay Company's standing instruction to its agents:

"Give as much as two years' credit to a wild pagan Indian—

but as soon as he cuts his hair and pretends he is civilized don't trust him, even overnight."

For a crime conforming to the sophisticated standards with which a European culture has made us familiar we have to move eastward to the Blue Ridge Mountains in1879.

The North Carolina hill folk had gathered together on this particular morning for a burial. The dead girl, Kathy Feller, had long been regarded as a semi-invalid, unfitted for the rough life of a farm wife.

Kathy suffered from chronic asthma, so it was no surprise to the neighbors when her husband, George Feller, woke them one morning with the news that she was having an unusually violent attack. He warned them that he feared for Kathy's life, so it was not much more of a surprise for them to find her already dead when they went to give help.

At the sight of his wife's body lying there, with their baby sleeping peacefully on the bed beside her, George Feller gave way to uncontrollable grief. His sympathetic neighbors took over the funeral preparations. The women laid out the body as was customary. The men constructed a board coffin.

So it came about that the little procession was following a wagon carrying the coffin to the grave made ready in the tiny mountain cemetery.

They had covered about half the four-mile distance, at a slow pace suited to the rough terrain and the solemn occasion, when they sighted a horseman blocking the roadway.

He lifted his hand in a signal to halt as they drew near. In a community where everyone was known to everyone else, the rider was a stranger. He was middle-aged and respectable in appearance, but his first words came as a shock.

"You can't bury this woman," he said. "She was murdered."

The mourners were as angry as they were startled. How could the stranger know that the coffin held the body of a woman, let alone the manner of her dying?

The stranger quietly gave his explanation. "I live over in Yancey County. I dreamed last night that riding into McDowell I would meet up with a funeral procession. The corpse in the coffin would be a woman's, murdered by her husband."

At their outcry he eased himself in the saddle, saying, "Now I don't know any of you folks. You don't know me. But you are the people I saw in my sleep. I saw the wagon and I saw the coffin."

George Feller, sitting up with the wagon driver, had said not a word. His neighbors, eyeing him, found this strange. They talked the matter over excitedly, but kept their voices low.

The stranger seemed sincere and talked convincingly. These people believed in dreams—of the symbolic sort that had to be interpreted. This one, if true, was awesomely specific.

Even so the majority were ready to disregard it. They knew young George Feller. Kathy could have died during any of her attacks, so why be suspicious? Someone reminded them again that the stranger had known it was a woman's body that was in the coffin. Maybe it was this, maybe the stranger's calm threat, that was the clinching argument.

"If you don't have her seen by a doctor," he warned, "I'm going to report it to the law."

They were still of the opinion that it was foolishness. But Kathy hadn't been seen by a doctor before she died anyway. So if only to prevent talk and rumor that could go on for years, the sensible thing was to humor him.

George Feller did argue a little against the decision. Natural feeling called for it, and George did not take his protest far enough to arouse suspicion. He was overruled, and the mourning procession turned and headed for the county seat at Marion.

The doctor had no doubt about the cause of death after he had seen the body. Kathy had been strangulated by outside pressure. Her asthmatic condition might have meant that less pressure on the neck was required than would be needed to stop the breathing of a person in good health, but that was the most it had to do with her dying.

The sheriff and the justice of the peace drove out to the Feller home in a buggy. Kathy had not been throttled manually; there were no marks of bruising. They were looking for something flat and smooth. They found it in a wooden chest in the bedroom— a broad band of rawhide. Clinging to it were a few hairs, long and golden, like Kathy's.

George Feller, who had acted surly and confused when the

sheriff first questioned him and put him in jail, collapsed when he was confronted with the length of rawhide.

He confessed that he and Kathy had had a row, going on and on into the night . . . until in the end he lost control and garrotted her with the rawhide strap. He had thought the neighbors would believe his story of how she had died. They had seen her struggling for breath before in her asthmatic attacks.

Of course, they did believe him; and the evidence of his crime would have been safely buried had it not been for the intervention of the psychic stranger.

George Feller, found guilty of murder, was the last man to be hanged in McDowell County.

Life, even out West, was not grim all the time. James Mathers began practicing law in Oklahoma when it was still a part of Indian Territory, and a natural hideout for outlaws. The James, the Younger, the Dalton and the Doolin gangs all operated from there at one time or another. Mathers himself was a member of the posse that killed Bill Dalton, last of the four outlaw brothers. He never entered court not wearing a gun, and in his time was involved with more cases carrying the death penalty—over a thousand—than any other lawyer.

But if crime can ever be lighthearted then an incident recalled in Judge Mathers' biography, *From Gun to Gavel,* certainly was.

Tim Ihland, blacksmith in the little town of Purcell, was a powerful, black-haired, black-bearded man of around fifty. His wife, Sarah, was a bit of a shrew, but they seemed happy enough. They had two children, young Tim who was twenty, and Maria, seventeen or so.

The nearest neighbors to the Ihlands were Martha Gray and her daughter, Sally. It was a mystery why Sally had not married. She was attractive enough, and at twenty-three was near to being an old maid by frontier standards.

Evidently, Tim the blacksmith had the problem of Sally in mind. One day a letter came from Lexington addressed to Sally. The Ihlands originated from Kentucky, and the writer introduced himself as Tim's nephew. He had heard about Sally's charms from Uncle Tim, he said, and was daring to propose a pen friendship. Sally, feeling lonely, was not averse to the idea. For the next eighteen months their correspondence flourished mightily, the letters from Lexington becoming increasingly amorous.

Came the proposal of marriage, which Sally accepted.

Ihlands and Grays were delighted at the prospect of the two families becoming more closely united. When Martha Gray published an announcement of the coming nuptials the town rejoiced with her. Showers were given for the bride, friends helped to sew her trousseau. All were agog for the day when Tim's nephew would arrive for the wedding.

There was a minor disappointment two days before the big event was due. Uncle Tim Ihland, after having so successfully played Cupid in the affair, announced that he had to go over to McAlester. One of his best customers had sent for him in an emergency. He hoped to be back in time for the wedding, but if he couldn't make it they had his good wishes. In any event he would see the happy couple before they left for Kentucky where they were planning to set up home.

Even without Uncle Tim to perform introductions the meeting went well. Sally was a mite nervous, but she had the support of her mother and the Ihlands. The nephew was as shy as Sally, and had little to say. In appearance he was a fine, upstanding fellow, with a neat red beard and red hair. Except for the matter of coloring, and two gold teeth that gleamed in his smile, he bore a striking likeness to Uncle Tim, as everybody remarked. Not feeling so good after his long trip, he kept to his room at the Ihlands most of the time before the wedding.

It was one of the finest weddings Purcell had ever known, marred only by Uncle Tim's unavoidable absence.

Tim had not returned when the newly-wedded pair were due to leave town.

Then a week, two weeks, three weeks went by, and Tim Ihland was still missing. By that time Sarah Ihland had drawn the obvious conclusion—Tim and his nephew were the same person!

It was Sarah's daughter, Maria, who put her on the track of the runaways. Maria was a medium, though most of her friends laughed about it. However, she did better than to vaguely confirm her mother's suspicions. She stated that her father and Sally Gray were living in Holdenville. Maria had never been there, but she could describe the location of their house.

Three or four blocks north of the depot, she said, were a trio of houses with white picket fences round the fronts. Her bigamous father had rented the one in the middle.

Sarah Ihland took the train to Holdenville. She walked up the street from the depot until she saw the three houses as Maria had pictured them. So scared was Sarah by the vision having thus far proved true that she almost ran back to the station.

She resisted the impulse, and then something forced her steps to the door of the middle house. It was opened to her knock by an equally shaken Sally Gray.

Sally admitted, in the face of Sarah's accusations, she had long ago discovered that she was married to "Uncle" Tim. At first she had stayed because she felt too embarrassed to return home, and now she was in love with him. Under Sarah's persuasion she eventually agreed they should go back together, and swear out a bigamy complaint.

When he was brought in by the marshal, Tim asked James Mathers to represent him. He had plenty of friends willing to sign as sureties for his thousand-dollar bail.

The court session had started, though Tim's case, being at the bottom of the list, had not been reached, when Mathers was called to the Ihland home. He went thinking Sarah must be intending to drop the charges.

He found her in the living room, with Tim junior. The boy looked pale as death. Sarah was nonchalantly getting supper ready.

Haltingly, young Tim told his story. That afternoon he had gone hunting wild turkey with his father, by the Canadian River. Sighting a bird on the opposite bank young Tim had fired, and thought he had killed it. His father, leaving his gun and coat behind, swam over to get the bird. Halfway across the river old Tim sank. Young Tim did not see him surface again. After searching along the bank for two hours, seeing no sign of his father, he had reported to the marshal's office.

Cross-examining the boy, Mathers became convinced he was telling the truth. His story stood up equally well in court, and by then the river had been dragged for three days without any trace being found of the body. The judge dismissed the bigamy action, and discharged the bondsmen.

Years later, when James Mathers had been elevated to the bench, Ben Lightfoot, an old Chickasaw whose reputation as a tracker was legendary, told him what he had seen the afternoon Tim Ihland disappeared.

On the way to set a trotline he had noticed two sets of footprints of white men going to the edge of the river. One man had entered the water, the other had done a lot of moving up and down the bank.

Then, several hundred yards downstream, Ben had seen the footprints of the man who went into the water again, this time coming out. Ben had never reported the matter. White man's business was no concern of an Indian.

On his next visit to Purcell, Judge Mathers inquired after Sarah Ihland. She was at the same house, he was told, and he called to see her. After a while Sarah admitted she knew that Tim was still alive, and living in Lexington with Sally Gray. Just as he had planned it.

Sarah had not been in touch with Tim, nor had she talked to anyone who had. Maria, she explained, had told her about it— just as she had given her information about his hideaway at Holdenville. And she had been right about that!

But, Sarah confessed, before Tim "drowned" she had agreed to let him go his own way, and if he did she would never want to see him again.

Sympathize as we will with Sarah in her domestic tragedy, we can yet admire the audacity of Tim Ihland, the husband who would have got clean away at the first try had his daughter not been a medium.

And, dragged back in disgrace, won clear again with a bit of persuasive blarney and an ingenuity that diddled the law.

CHAPTER TEN

□

The Law and the Prophets

ACTING as an *agent provocateur* a policewoman attended a gathering of the League of Quiet Helpers at Worthing, Sussex. A psychometry meeting was being held that afternoon. Each visitor placed a small personal article on a tray put out in readiness. Later the medium, handling the objects one by one, gave the owner a "reading." The fee was a shilling.

The policewoman's turn came round. Among other things, the medium told her, "I see you surrounded by men in blue." Her civilian dress had given no clue to her calling, and if this was a psychic impression it could not be faulted on accuracy.

Yet the next thing the hapless medium knew she was at the police station, surrounded by men in blue herself, being charged with pretending to tell fortunes. Once again the law had made an ass of itself.

Ever since Jesus of Nazareth was charged with doing good works—which probably meant exercising the spiritual gifts afterwards listed by St. Paul—a descending line of lesser prophets, dedicated mediums, hopeful self-deceivers and absolute rogues have been lumped together under the law and persecuted. In modern England it was the usually harmless, mainly honest, back-street mediums in provincial towns who came in for most attention.

The society clairvoyants operating discreetly on the fringes (some in the heart) of Mayfair and Kensington, the crystal gazers and card readers blatantly advertising themselves along Oxford Street and Charing Cross Road, the Romany seers and astrologers at holiday resorts circling the coasts of Britain, were seldom, if ever, troubled by the police.

English law, up to 1951, made no distinction between the genuine and the fraudulent. Even when the police were forced to admit that what the medium had told them was true, that was no defense, against *pretense*. At a logical level this was the same as maintaining that a sober man who has a motor accident is a drunken driver. Fraudulent mediums could be found; but it took a little more effort than a visit to the Spiritualist church round the corner to arrest the first medium in sight. All, or nearly all, the prosecutions for serious fraud I can recollect, have been the result of exposure by Spiritualists or psychical researchers themselves, not by the police. Some of the fakes I have known personally are dealt with in an earlier book.*

Here I am concerned with the role genuine mediums may play by, so to speak, looking over the shoulder of the law when occasion arises.

Spirit guidance is not all exhortation and uplift. It can be very practical. Neither should we assume that when the recent dead return, their sole interest is the spiritual welfare of those left behind. Sometimes their attention is given to most material affairs.

Denis Conan Doyle, son of Sir Arthur, the creator of Sherlock Holmes and a foremost champion of Spiritualism, recalled a séance with his parents and, among others, a Scottish engineer named John Gregory. One of the communicators claimed to be Gregory's dead wife. She told him she had left £400 in a bank account, to which he was legally entitled though it was not mentioned in her will.

Gregory wrote to the bank she had named. There was no such account, they replied.

When his wife spoke again at the next séance, Gregory told her what the bank had said. She insisted she was right, and urged him to write again.

Gregory made a second inquiry. This time he received a letter

* *Exploring the Psychic World.*

apologizing for the previous blunder. The account which had been overlooked did hold the sum of £400.

A well-known London medium, William Redmond, was able to help a woman who was involved in a complicated law suit following the death of her husband. At séances with Redmond detailed advice on what she should do, and how she should do it, came from the husband. If she carried out the instructions, he predicted, she would win the case.

The widow believed him. "You see, Mr. Redmond," she explained, "my husband was a lawyer. He is an expert in this kind of litigation—that's how I know it is my husband speaking. If he says I will win, you can be sure I shall." And happily she did.

If we dismiss from our minds the traditional idea of the dead occupying themselves with playing harps and choir-singing, it seems natural enough that a lawyer should retain his interest in the law, and particularly in safeguarding his own family from its pitfalls.

A Miss Dallas had her will drawn by her uncle, a solicitor, who subsequently died. She went, anonymously, to a private sitting with a medium, and the uncle was described to her. She was reminded that he had drawn up a document for her, perhaps a will. Of course, she knew all this. The surprise was what followed.

There was something wrong, the medium said, with the document. It was not wholly wrong, but it did contain an error.

Miss Dallas went home and reread the will. She could find no fault. So she went to a solicitor and asked him to examine it.

He gave his opinion that as a legal document it was perfectly in order. The only doubt was whether her intentions had been correctly interpreted.

Her main capital, consisting of railway shares, Miss Dallas explained, she wanted divided among her relatives.

In that case, the solicitor said, the will was certainly in error. She owned two different kinds of railway shares. Only one of them had been specified in the will. As it stood the major holding would not go to her relatives, but to the residuary legatee.

Miss Dallas had the will redrafted.

Few circumstances are more mentally distressing, one imagines, than to be arraigned in court for a crime of which one is innocent. In this kind of situation words of spiritual comfort are all very well, but reassurance is increased a hundredfold if evidence comes with it that the "everything will be all right" talk is based on real knowledge of what is to come.

On January 2, 1950, Mrs. E. Johnson was at her home in Southwest London, entertaining a friend. She had just poured cups of coffee when she heard a knock. She opened the door, and there were two men standing outside.

They said they were police officers. Acting on information received—that phrase so familiar in every police court—they had called to see if she could assist them with their inquiries into the theft of two pairs of gloves from Harvey Nichols, the well-known store in Knightsbridge.

She said she had no idea what they were talking about.

The detectives elaborated. Some woman had visited the store and selected eight pairs of gloves, requesting that they be charged to her account. Six pairs could be delivered, she said; the other two pairs she would take with her.

She took them while the shop assistant was checking on the account, which proved to be nonexistent.

The police had reason to believe that Mrs. Johnson was that woman.

She protested her innocence. She invited them to search the flat, but they refused. What they had come for was to invite her, firmly, to accompany them to the police station to take part in an identification parade.

Mrs. Johnson agreed to go with them. The first shock having worn off, she was quite confident. She knew she had not been in Harvey Nichols for years.

It was a stunning blow when a store detective and a shop assistant picked her out of the lineup.

This was after the police had kept Mrs. Johnson waiting six hours for the identification parade to be arranged. In that time she had learned that the theft took place three weeks before, on December 7.

It so happened that she could remember her movements on that day quite clearly. Her son-in-law had been taking an accountancy examination, and that stamped the date on her memory. At the hour she was supposed to have been robbing Harvey

Nichols she was at home with her hair in curlers doing house-
work.

The police would not accept her story. She was charged and
told to appear in court next day. When the case was called
Mrs. Johnson's solicitor asked for a remand so that counsel
could be briefed. This was granted, with bail set at £20.

The next day Mrs. Johnson went to see Lilian Bailey, one of
the finest trance mediums in Britain, and a woman of charm and
intelligence.

Mrs. Johnson had had séances with her before, but Mrs. Bailey
had no idea of the reason for this unexpected visit, though it was
easy to deduce that she was in some kind of trouble.

When Mrs. Bailey went into trance, however, her control, Bill
Wootton, came quickly to the point. "We know what happened,"
he assured Mrs. Johnson. "Ted was in court with you yesterday.
So was your daughter, Molly, and others of your dead relations."

He referred to Mrs. Johnson being out on £20 bail—the spirits
seemed to find it amusing. Then, more sympathetically, Wootton
said: "We know your distress, but don't worry. We know you
are innocent. It is a case of mistaken identity. It is all over two
pairs of gloves which you are supposed to have stolen from
Harvey Nichols."

All this, naturally, was very much to the forefront of Mrs.
Johnson's mind. If such accurate and detailed telepathy were possible, that could be the explanation. The next remark through
the lips of the entranced medium falls in a different category.

"They are also going to try to accuse you of taking gloves from
another well-known store." Mrs. Johnson knew nothing of this.
Such an additional charge did come up later, but it was dropped
before reaching the court stage.

Not much reassurance was given. Indeed, Bill Wootton warned
Mrs. Johnson that she was not to expect much sympathy at the
magistrate's court.

She appeared before Mr. Paul Bennett, V.C., at Marlborough
Street. All the witnesses had not been heard when the magistrate
decided there would not be time to finish the case that day, and
it was adjourned until the following week.

In the interim Mrs. Johnson again visited Lilian Bailey.

Her immediate future, as outlined by Bill Wootton, was not

rosy. He told her that despite her protestations of innocence the magistrate would convict her when she next appeared in court.

Naturally she found this grim prediction upsetting, but then came a more cheerful forecast. She should appeal, Wootton said, and then she would go before three judges, one of whom would be named Hawke. They would set her free, and she would be given compensation.

Wootton went into details about what would happen at the appeal. One of the judges would laugh when reference to a bus journey came up in evidence. He would make a joke about Mrs. Johnson's handwriting. On the morning of the appeal it would be very foggy, but by around midday when the case was over the sun would shine.

Everything happened as Wootton had prophesied. Although Mrs. Johnson had witnesses to support her alibi, the evidence of the store detective and the shop assistant was accepted by the magistrate. She was sentenced to two months' imprisonment.

Her counsel, Eric Neve, K.C., gave notice of appeal, and bail was allowed in the same sum as before.

When Mrs. Johnson again saw Lilian Bailey the date for the appeal to be heard had not been settled. Bill Wootton told her what day it would be, and she found he was right. Two cases would be tried before hers, he added. Her case would begin at about 11 A.M.

The morning of the appeal was foggy. Mrs. Johnson reached court, and had to wait for two other cases to be dealt with.

The chairman of the judges was Mr. Anthony Hawke. When Mrs. Johnson gave evidence he asked her how long it would take to reach Harvey Nichols by bus, from the stop nearest to her door. She guessed, about ten minutes.

The judge laughed, saying it would take him longer. Obviously he knew the route, for he gave his own estimate as at least fifteen minutes.

Counsel asked Mrs. Johnson to write the name "MacRoberts" on a sheet of foolscap which was handed to her. When her effort was passed to the judge he smiled again on seeing her overlarge handwriting. She must use up a lot of notepaper, he joked.

The appeal tribunal stopped the case before Mrs. Johnson had called all her witnesses, allowing the appeal and granting costs.

When, at midday, Mrs. Johnson walked out of the courthouse a free woman, the fog had cleared. The sun, real as well as symbolic, was brightly shining.

It should be noted that there was nothing generalized and indefinite about these messages. Such trivia as the jokes from the bench may not be relevant to the result, but are more calculated to give a distressed victim of judicial error confidence than a weak assurance that things will be well. The guide demonstrated that he really did have advance knowledge of what was going to happen.

The outcome of the trial was similarly predicted when James Caunt, editor of the *Morecambe and Heysham Visitor,* was charged with publishing a seditious libel.

Two weeks before the case came to court a medium, Frank Spencer, was giving a demonstration of clairvoyance at Nottingham. He picked out a woman in the audience, and described to her a dead relative he said was connected with a newspaper in his lifetime.

"He says that Jim, who is now running the paper, has done or written something which has caused a terrible row. I get the name Morecambe—does that mean anything to you?"

The woman nodded that she understood.

"There will be a big law case," the medium continued. "It will attract a lot of publicity. Things will appear very gruesome for a time, but Jim will get through."

Not so definite in detail, maybe, but the meaning seemed plain.

The woman receiving the message was Mrs. Alec Leary, a resident of Nottingham. Before her marriage she had been a Miss Caunt, and could surmise that the communicator was her uncle, the former owner and editor of the *Visitor.* At his death his son, Jim, Mrs. Leary's cousin, had taken over the paper.

The medium could have known, as did Mrs. Leary, that an action against the Morecambe newspaper was pending. But he had no apparent means of knowing that a woman closely related to the editor would be in his audience at a city a hundred miles away.

The trial ended with James Caunt winning his discharge.

Spiritualists are no more litigious-minded than most, possibly less. Occasionally, however, the question of copyright in artistic works allegedly communicated from the spirit world has given rise to entertaining mix-ups.

Noel Rosa, Brazil's favorite composer of sambas, dictated verses after his death to Herve Cordovil, his former collaborator. Cordovil set the verses to music, but when a popular singer wanted to record the song he refused permission. An ardent Spiritualist himself, Cordovil thought he had no right to authorize the song being performed commercially until the spirit of Rosa had communicated his agreement.

Unhappily, from this point of view, he had allowed the Rosa lyrics to be published in *Porvir,* a Spiritualist periodical, and a Rio de Janeiro newspaper had the bright idea to run a competition for setting them to music.

When a young amateur composer, Maria Tersinha, won the competition, Noel Rosa's widow was persuaded to sign a contract allowing the lyrics to be used.

The question then facing the Brazilian Society of Music Composers, Authors and Writers, was who owned the copyright: Herve Cordovil, who had written down the lyrics at Noel Rosa's spirit dictation; or Doña Laurinda, Rosa's widow and heiress?

Sehnor Ary Barroso, president of the Society, was of the opinion that Noel, as a spirit, was not married and had no heirs.

His verdict was in line with an urbane judgment delivered by Mr. Justice Eve, which resolved the matter of spirit copyright so far as English law is concerned. The occasion was a dispute between the Reverend Frederick Bligh Bond and Geraldine Cummins, the famous automatist.

Bligh Bond, an ecclesiastical architect and archaeologist, rediscovered the lost chapels at Glastonbury Abbey. He was guided in his excavations by automatic scripts received through several mediums.

He contended that writings for which Miss Cummins was amanuensis would not have been communicated without the special mental link he provided as the sitter. Mr. Justice Eve gave judgment in favor of the medium being sole author in law of anything written by her hand, no matter to whom the writings were addressed or by what minds she might be influenced.

The possible claims of real ghost writers, he decided, were outside his jurisdiction.

CHAPTER ELEVEN

□

Not "Private Eyes" but "Psychic Eyes"

WHAT is a "hunch"? A nudge from the subconscious, or a hint from Elsewhere? And intuition? Just jumping to conclusions, or an extrasensory springboard to truth?

Even so eminent a skeptic as Bernard Shaw told me of odd personal experiences he regarded as examples of telepathy. For example, he might suddenly think of someone he had not heard from in years, with no particular reason for bringing them to mind at that moment. Next day he would receive a letter from the person.

This kind of experience is fairly common. It impresses people when it happens to them—and I include famous professional doubters other than G.B.S.—perhaps rather more than it should. To assess such cases properly one would need to know how often a person had popped into mind with no subsequent letter arriving, and have means of ruling out any unconnected stimuli which could have pushed the person into the conscious.

Nevertheless, if we accept extrasensory perception—and the evidence is overwhelming—then spontaneous phenomena of this order very likely do occur. Indeed, a similar apparent spontaneity is a characteristic of many kinds of psychic experience. The medium achieves a special relaxation by native talent and training. Psychic impressions come to others most often when they are in a relaxed frame of mind, in everyday activities or circumstances, or drowsing into sleep, even in the guise of a dream.

Men usually call it a hunch, women claim it as intuition.

There is no reason why detectives should be immune to psychic impressions. Take the case of one of Britain's top policemen, ex-Deputy Commander William Rawlings, C.B.E., M.C., of New Scotland Yard.

While he was C.I.D. Inspector at the Sutton subdivision of "W" division, he was one day called to investigate a burglary. He found only two possible clues: a bus ticket he picked up in the house, and a piece of red ribbon hanging from the garden hedge.

His questioning eliminated the possibility of the bus ticket having been dropped by anyone living in the house. The ribbon was identified by the householder as having come from a box of chocolates given her by her husband. The thief had taken the chocolates as well as some articles of jewelry.

The chocolate box was the kind of clue a fiction writer might have dreamed up—and then hesitated to use. The lady's husband, it appeared, presented her with a box of chocolates every weekend. Somewhere on the box he always wrote the words, "I love you." The romantic game was to find the message, for it might be anywhere, inside or outside the box. Sometimes he took the trouble to remove all the sweets and replace them after writing underneath, so that the three important little words would not be revealed until the chocolates were almost finished.

Rawlings asked his witness if she had seen a message on the stolen box. No, she had not, though she had already eaten the first of the two layers.

Next day Rawlings put in some outstanding work of detection. The bus ticket he traced to a route running across "M" division, which was Southwark. A punch mark indicated the fare stage.

Rawlings boarded a bus and bought a ticket. It did not match the other. He showed the used ticket to the conductor, who was able to tell him the right bus to take and, most valuable, where the fare stage was at which the traveler would have alighted.

In a police car Rawlings followed the bus route at a crawl. He was trying to pick out one man from the ceaseless stream of pedestrians. Hundreds of them were likely to fit the only description he had, supplied by neighbors of the burgled household, of a man who might have been the thief. He had called at several houses asking if they had brass ornaments to sell.

The sergeant driving the car obviously doubted Rawlings' sanity in playing such a way-out hunch.

They saw no one who looked suspicious in the slightest along the route. The fare stage to which the ticket extended was at Lambeth Bridge. They began to work back from there, this time stopping at the pubs on the way.

At the first two pubs they entered they were out of luck. They pulled up at a third, and went in separately. Each had ordered his half-pint of beer when two young people, a man and a woman, came in.

The inspector and the sergeant started to chat as if they were pub acquaintances. The young man fitted the description of the burglar but, as the sergeant pointed out, so would a lot more people. Rawlings had his hunch.

The couple sat down, ordered drinks and began talking. Rawlings, half a dozen yards away, thought he heard the man say, "It was easy." He could have meant the burglary the day before —or a thousand other things. Experience warned Rawlings to hold his imagination in check, but he somehow felt convinced that this was his man.

A moment later the man was showing the girl something which she took, held against her coat, and then slipped into her handbag. Was it a piece of stolen jewelry?

She returned the handbag to her shopping basket, and then Rawlings really became excited. She had brought out a box of chocolates!

Common sense told him what fantastic odds were against it being the box he was looking for; but an unknown something nagged at his mind as persistently.

He went over to look at a picture on the wall behind where the couple were sitting. He passed a comment on it to the landlord, who said it depicted the finish of that year's Derby. That caused the suspect to look up at it, and Rawlings had the chance to bring him into the conversation.

He was able to glance down at the box of chocolates on the table. They were the same brand as the stolen box. Some were missing from the last layer, but where the bottom showed he could not see any writing. He joked with the girl about her liking for chocolates, said he had a sweet tooth himself, and cheekily asked if he could have one.

She offered the box. Rawlings thanked her and dipped in. He shuffled the chocolates around, pretending to be looking for a special kind. The man muttered that he was being "bloody choosy."

But by then Rawlings had seen two words, "I" and "you". He moved a few chocolates to cover them again.

Inside the pub he had no power to search and hold a suspect. But the law allowed him to do so in the street if he had reasonable cause to believe that something stolen was being carried.

He waited for the young couple to leave the pub. Outside, while they were waiting to board a bus, Rawlings and the sergeant approached them, and asked to see the chocolates. On the bottom of the box was written the complete phrase, "I love you."

The man exonerated the girl, admitting he had given her both chocolates and jewelry.

At a later stage in his career, when he was Divisional Detective Inspector of "F" division, which covered Millionaires' Row —Kensington Palace Gardens—as well as the criminal purlieus of Notting Dale, Rawlings was again somehow guided to the right spot at the right time.

The elderly landlady of a lodging house off Shepherd's Bush Green was found tied up in her basement, dead. Two lodgers, who had vanished at the same time, were the obvious suspects.

The case became a classic manhunt. The B.B.C. broadcast an appeal to landladies to report any man and woman answering the descriptions given, who had registered since the date of the murder. This brought 244 replies, and each had to be investigated.

The stock ticket from a garment found in the house was traced to a shop at Hammersmith. The shop people identified it as having been attached to a costume sold to a young woman, who for some reason had given the name of the murdered landlady when she bought it. An observant assistant remembered the purchaser because the skirt had had to be shortened.

As Rawlings left the shop, deep in thought, he was snapped by a street photographer, and a card pushed into his hand.

This gave him an idea—maybe the girl had been photographed by the same man when she bought the costume. He knew the date of the sale. He borrowed the negatives of all the films taken that day from the photographic studio.

Then he held a picture show at Scotland Yard. His hopes were dashed when his witnesses failed to recognize the girl in any of the photographs.

Rawlings did not give up. He sent for all the snapshots taken in the succeeding week.

He had shown over 7,300 photographs, and there were not many left, when the witnesses picked out both the girl and the man with her on the snap, as the missing lodgers.

So that their testimony should not be weakened, Rawlings had to discard any thought of publishing a photograph in the newspapers. Copies could be issued only to the police. Luck was with him . . . the couple were identified as a married man and a single girl who, several months before, had run away together from their homes in Stepney.

Their capture was heralded when the girl made the mistake of writing to her mother. The letter was postmarked "London E.8."—the opposite side of London from Shepherd's Bush.

Rawlings made plans to comb the E.8 area, a busy working-class district, on a Saturday when he thought the wanted pair—the man coming home from work, the girl going shopping?—would most likely be on the streets. He could muster only fifty men and one patrol car. On the face of it this was a try at long odds.

Dalston police station was his headquarters when the operation got under way. Around lunch time, Rawlings left to go to a nearby chemist to get bismuth for his ulcer. The sun having suddenly become much warmer, he turned back to leave his overcoat in the office. When he came out a second time he decided, inexplicably, to walk to the crossroads where people were queueing for buses.

A bus drew up as he approached. He watched the passengers alighting, and then the pain in his stomach was forgotten . . . among them was the man in the photograph.

As Rawlings caught sight of him the man turned, pushing his way back into the bus. Rawlings jumped on the bus, forcing a path after him . . . but the man was already coming back, with a newspaper-wrapped parcel he must have forgotten.

He was the killer all right, but he cut a pitiful figure. The robbery of the landlady had netted him only ten pounds. He was reduced to doing casual work at Billingsgate Fish Market for wages that barely paid the rent. The parcel he had gone back to collect contained leftover scraps of fish he had picked up to provide himself and the girl with a meal.

What turned Rawlings away from the pharmacy and led him to the bus stop just when the suspect was about to arrive? In films and novels, of course, it has to be the leading character who is placed in the path of the villain at the climactic moment. Here fifty men, all with the same chance of making an arrest, were combing the area. Yet some "hunch" impelled Rawlings, whose main job was to direct rather than to search, to go to the vital spot at the right fraction of time.

The explanation of these experiences must be left with a question mark. In his memoirs, *A Case for the Yard,* Ex-Deputy Commander Rawlings offers no firm opinion concerning them. The inspiration that guided Detective Frank P. Geyer to the solution of a shooting in Philadelphia came in much more explicit fashion.

The victim, Annie Klaus, was a young girl who worked in a stocking factory—and that was about all she did outside the home. Sex was the only motive for her killing that made sense, but the trouble was that Annie knew no men. Every minute of her day was strictly accounted for, and the possibility of a lover just could not fit in.

Then, at the murdered girl's home, Geyer experienced a strange awareness of her being present. "I am the last man in the world to believe in intuition, or to form a theory on nothing," he said later, "but I saw the girl as though she were pictured on a canvas screen, looking out of the old stocking mill window and flirting with the conductors of the old green line whose cars came down Canal Street."

He began to check on the car crews. His suspicions eventually centered on an albino conductor. The day Geyer went to the man's home to make an arrest the conductor cut his wife's throat, then his own. Fortunately, the wife recovered.

Geyer summed up the case: "It seems to me that the only way it could possibly have been solved was by that flash of intuition that pictured to me the fresh young face of Annie Klaus at the mill window, as she flirted with the crews of the cars going past."

There are degrees of experience. Still more vivid was the dream warning that came to Detective Inspector "Mac" McLaughlan, of the political division of the Special Branch at Scotland Yard.

This was at a time of political unrest in India. Agitators aimed to terrorize the politicians in London with threats of violence. Detective Inspector McLaughlan's job was to keep an eye on the agitators, and one who came particularly to his attention was Madar Lal Dhingra.

Not all the known activists were dangerous—perhaps very few would ever try to implement their more violent threats. McLaughlan was certain that if there was a dangerous man among them it was Lal Dhingra. His name was at the top of the list McLaughlan sent to Sir Curzon Wyllie, political aide to the Secretary of State for India.

On a night in May, 1909, McLaughlan had a dream. In the dream he saw Lal Dhingra standing near a group of large buildings with a revolver in his hand.

Several nights later the dream recurred, with an added detail. McLaughlan now recognized the main building as a government office.

A week went by and McLaughlan dreamed again. The scene was as before but events had progressed a stage further. He saw Lal Dhingra firing the revolver at some person in a crowd.

In June, McLaughlan received information that the young Indian had indeed acquired a revolver. Armed with a search warrant he made a surprise visit to Lal Dhingra, but did not succeed in finding the gun either in his room or on his person.

The detective was worried for by then it was known that a reception of great splendor was to be held on July 1 at the Imperial Institute. Sir Curzon Wyllie was to attend. McLaughlan was prepared for trouble.

The day arrived; and McLaughlan, reporting at the Yard, found himself transferred to other duties. When he protested, he was told to follow orders; no other ranking officer was available for the job he was being given.

At nine o'clock that night, while McLaughlan was hunting criminals elsewhere, Wyllie and one of his closest friends, Dr. Cawas Lalcacca, a Parsee physician, left the reception hall at the Imperial Institute. Surrounded by a group of people they had reached the top of the stairway when Lal Dhingra rushed forward and fired five shots. Wyllie, struck in the head, fell to the ground.

Dr. Lalcacca leapt to grapple with the assassin. Lal Dhingra, with his remaining bullet, shot the Parsee dead.

Before he went off duty McLaughlan heard the news. "I walked away from the Yard that night in a trance," he said afterwards. "It had all appeared so vividly to me."

Not every psychic warning to detectives ends in disaster. In the files of Dr. J. B. Rhine, of Duke University—who has done more than anyone to establish experimental proof of extrasensory perception—is a dramatic instance of a warning with a happy result.

One morning an insurance investigator was awakened by a friend, a member of the police force. It was 4 A.M.—and the caller looked as if he had seen a ghost.

"Lend me your gun," he begged urgently.

The insurance investigator handed over his .44 Smith and Wesson. He was the more puzzled when the police officer gave him his own Colt .38 in exchange, with the warning, "For God's sake, don't carry it. I can't tell you why. You would think I was crazy."

Six hours later—10 A.M.—the insurance investigator had a phone call from a hospital. His friend had walked into a holdup. He had killed two hoodlums and wounded a third with five shots from the Smith and Wesson before receiving the slight chest wound that had put him in the hospital.

The investigator called round to see him. The police officer had a strange request—he wanted him to go to the police practice range and test the Colt he had left with him.

Puzzled but willing to oblige, his friend did what he asked. The gun fired perfectly well at the first shot . . . the second. . . . On the third shot the spring failed, rendering the weapon useless. This kind of mechanical failure is very rare with a modern revolver; but it had happened.

And when he reported back to the police officer in the hospital he was not surprised. "I thought it would," he said, with grim satisfaction. "I dreamt I was in a gun fight, and my gun failed on the third shot."

So real and urgent an impression had the dream had upon him that he knew he must find another weapon before he went on duty.

"I was even scared," he confessed, "to drive the two and a half blocks to your place with that Colt."

The dream may have saved his life. Five bullets had been needed to beat off the bandits.

Of course, very few professional detectives practice clairvoyance regularly. One who does—almost routinely, one might say—is Fred Liston, former senior investigator for the NAAFI Special Investigation Department with the British forces in Germany.

Apart from its usefulness in his work, Liston's clairvoyant gift has impressed many of his friends in the police and the legal profession, who vouch for its accuracy.

One solicitor consulted Liston when he was having great difficulty in tracing an important will that was missing. The detective told him where to find it, but added that it was valueless because it had never been signed. He proved doubly right.

In his dealings with crooks, Liston has had notable psychic success. Once he was interviewing some seamen about stolen cigarettes. With nothing to go on except clairvoyance he suddenly said to a petty officer, "What about the cigarettes you put in the ashbin?"

It shocked the man into confessing that he had concealed no fewer than 10,000 cigarettes under the waste.

Another time hundreds of dollars worth of coffee substitute had been stolen from NAAFI stores in Hamburg. Liston had a vision of a man so important he would have been thought above suspicion, and with it a warning message to question a second man before directly investigating the first. This angle of approach resulted in both the thief and the receiver being exposed.

Like all mediums, Fred Liston finds that psychic power does not work all the time, nor can it be called upon at will. When the flashes do come they usually put him on the right track—the rest is hard, orthodox police work.

There was a famous detective whose premonition of murder came true. It did not prevent the crime nor help him solve it— though he did bring the culprit to book in the end.

The Frenchman, Robert Ledru, was so nearly a prototype of the ideal investigator that legends were woven around him while he was still a young man. It was said he could describe a man by examining his footprints, could identify a tobacco by smelling the ash.

Exaggerations were pardonable for Ledru was, indeed, the Holmesian type of detective who would painstakingly scrutinize the scene of a crime for the minutest clue; a man whose methods would gladden the hearts of laboratory criminologists today, who too often find that unthinking field investigators have failed to collect meaningful trivia.

Ledru worked hard, averaging only a few hours' sleep a night for long periods, until his health began to fail. His short slumbers were disturbed by fearful dreams in which he himself committed murder. His superiors at last prevailed upon him to take a vacation.

He went to Le Havre, and had not been there long when the Sûreté received report of a murder at Ste. Adresse, two miles farther along the coast.

Andre Monet, a businessman, on holiday with his wife, had fancied a late night swim before going to bed. In the morning a baker's delivery boy found Monet's nude body lying on the beach, above high water mark. He had been shot through the head.

It seemed providential to the officials in Paris that their most brilliant operative should be almost on the spot. They telegraphed at once that Ledru should take over the investigation.

There had been no robbery. The dead man's money and possessions were folded in with his clothes which were stacked near the body. Monet had no known enemies, and the only person to benefit financially from his death was his wife. Madame Monet, it was clearly established, had been in the hotel at the time her husband must have died.

Robert Ledru undertook one of his celebrated surveys of the scene of the crime. He had the area roped off, and began his usual careful search. He found his clue . . . a distinctive footprint. A plaster cast was taken.

The next day Ledru demonstrated with the plaster cast at police headquarters. He explained how the murderer, in stockinged feet, must have crept up behind his victim. The footprint was easily identifiable, he pointed out, because the first joint of the big toe was missing.

At that point Ledru bent and took off his shoe. He lifted his foot above the edge of the table.

"I am the murderer," he said resignedly, when his colleagues could see that he had a missing joint. "Now I know why my stockings were damp yesterday morning."

The crime was without motive. Ledru, reenacting his dreams, had simply shot an unlucky stranger—and had then solved the insoluble crime, though it meant his own exposure.

Medical testimony at his trial supported the plea that Ledru could be considered dangerous only at night while sleepwalking. Why then, his counsel pleaded, must the sane, waking man be executed?

The logic must have appealed to the French court for it passed a rare, possibly unique, sentence of nighttime imprisonment. For the rest of his long life, Robert Ledru's confinement was suspended every day from sunrise to sunset, when he was locked up again until the following morning. One night in 1939 he died in his cell.

□

CHAPTER TWELVE

Clairvoyant Crimebusters of Europe

ONE day in the autumn of 1946 a young coal miner came home from work as usual. He had reached his doorstep when two shots rang out, killing him instantly.

The Dutch police—this was at Limburg—were baffled. Not that a suspect was hard to find. The murdered man's stepfather, Bernard van Tossings, was known to have a jealous passion for his stepson's wife. What puzzled the police was to know where he had hidden the weapon, and without it their case was incomplete.

It was a bulky, black-haired, former house painter who advised, "Take a look at the roof of the murdered man's house."

There, lying in the rain gutter, the police found a revolver with two empty chambers. The elder Van Tossings' fingerprints were on the butt, assuring his conviction.

Deduction? Guesswork? As an isolated instance it could have been either. But this was only the start of Peter Hurkos' career as a psychic detective.

The police forces of Britain have seldom been willing to cooperate with a clairvoyant, and do not readily acknowledge aid when it has been given. In some European countries there is less reluctance to work with a medium; especially in Germany and Holland, whose policemen are often portrayed as being particularly stolid and down-to-earth!

Lotte Plaat, an outstanding Dutch medium, was regularly consulted by the German police as far back as the nineteen-twenties. Then when stories of psychic activities in this field began to reach me from Europe after the war, two names kept cropping up with increasing frequency—Peter Hurkos and Gerard Croiset. Both were Dutchmen and about the same age, middle thirties then. It is a minor mystery why Holland, a small country where there are few known mediums even moderately gifted, should produce the three sensitives who have most successfully specialized in criminal detection. Between them Hurkos and Croiset have helped the police of a dozen countries to the solution of murder, arson, theft and other crimes.

An outbreak of arson occurred in August, 1951, striking terror among the farmers living between Arnhem and Nijmegen, near the German border of Holland. Barns, hayricks and wagons were being destroyed overnight.

When a Nijmegen textile mill owner, Boy Sonneville, brought Peter Hurkos onto the scene, two hundred armed men were patrolling the area, and insurance investigators calculated that the damage had already mounted to £140,000.

"There will be another fire tonight," Hurkos predicted as he passed a gutted building. "At a farm near the city . . . owned by the Jansens."

Sonneville knew the Jansen farm. He hastened to take Hurkos to police headquarters. There, at first mention of the name Jansen, Police Captain Cammaert interrupted their recital. The fire brigade had been alerted half an hour before, and were already at the scene. Was Hurkos trying to pull a publicity stunt?

In order to convince the police chief, Hurkos began to itemize the contents of his pockets for him. This feat of X-ray vision persuaded Cammaert that Hurkos might have known about the fire without being told. He became more agreeable, and finally took Hurkos on a tour of the farms where outbreaks had occurred.

In a gutted building at the third farm they visited Hurkos stooped to pick up a screwdriver from the charred floor. He fingered it for a few minutes, then said, "We must look for a boy."

He wanted the police to bring him every photograph of local youths they could lay their hands on. They collected more than five hundred—from police files, school records and photographic studios. Hurkos then took over a room at police headquarters, and started a careful examination.

"This is the boy I want to talk to," he said finally.

Hurkos had picked out Piet Vierboom, seventeen-year-old son of a wealthy and highly respected Nijmegen family. The police were not happy about his choice.

But Hurkos was emphatic that young Vierboom was the culprit. When they found him, Hurkos said, he would be wearing blue overalls. In one of the pockets he would be carrying a box of matches, in another a bottle of lighter fluid. "But Piet does not smoke," he added.

Young Vierboom was repairing a bicycle tire in his father's garage. Hurkos was right about his dress, the matches and the lighter fluid. But the detectives retained their misgivings. Piet looked far too innocent and wholesome a lad for their peace of mind.

At police headquarters Hurkos talked to him, not accusingly but gently. "There are deep scratches on your leg—the left leg," he said. "You caught it on barbed wire, I think."

Piet was told to pull up his trouser leg. Scratches were revealed running from calf to thigh. He looked at Hurkos in frightened wonderment. "I cannot lie to you," he said, and thereupon made a full confession. After trial, he was committed to a mental institution.

In Occupied France during the war it was illegal for the private citizen to possess gold. The answer of many Frenchmen was to bury it. M. Delbeck-Dupont, a merchant of Roubaix, dug a hole in his vegetable garden, and in it secreted a tin box containing seventeen ingots and thirty-six gold coins.

When, in 1951, M. Delbeck-Dupont began to feel it might be safe to dig up his treasure it was too late. The gold had vanished.

The part played by Peter Hurkos in recovering the gold is vouched for by a top official of the Sûreté Nationale at Lille.

All Hurkos had to link him with the thief was the vegetable bed in which the gold had been buried. He concluded that the criminals were Lucien Durnez, a part-time gardener, and his father, Gerard. The gold had at first been hidden in their house, but had since been removed. Until it was found nothing would be gained by challenging them.

After a while Hurkos solved the problem. He led the way to a greenhouse, entered, and began digging in the flower boxes. From one of them he unearthed M. Delbeck-Dupont's tin full of gold.

Lucien Durnez, interrogated by the police, admitted having taken the gold. He had discovered it by accident, while removing old roots from the vegetable garden. As Hurkos had said, Durnez and his father had first kept it in the house, then later had thought to hide their booty in the greenhouse. Both were sentenced to six months' imprisonment and a fine of 25,000 francs.

Hurkos has no Spiritualistic beliefs, and claims to be as baffled as anyone else by his psychic abilities. He became aware of them in a peculiar fashion. One day in June, 1943, he was working with his father near The Hague. They were painting a school, and Peter had climbed to the top of a thirty-six-foot ladder when he slipped and fell.

He did not recover consciousness for three days, when he found himself in a bed at the Zuidwal Hospital with a fractured skull. Then, to his own astonishment, he heard himself saying to the patient in the next bed, "You are a bad man."

The other patient was Aard Camberg, a grocer. Puzzled, he asked Hurkos what he meant.

Camberg's father had died recently, Hurkos reminded him. "He left you a gold watch, and now you have sold it."

It was true—and both men knew they had never met each other before.

A nurse came into the ward. Hurkos immediately advised her to take care not to lose a valise belonging to a friend when she went on a train journey.

The nurse had just returned from Amsterdam to come on duty. She had left a friend's valise in the buffet car of the train.

Her reaction to Hurkos' astounding statement was to send for the hospital psychiatrist. The doctor could find nothing wrong with Hurkos apart from his physical injuries. His diagnosis was —extrasensory perception.

This did not comfort the patient, who now found that just being near to people or objects sent all kinds of disturbing images crowding into his mind. But when he left the hospital after nine weeks, with Holland still under enemy occupation, he found his new faculty could be put to good use. He was able to advise people what had become of relatives and friends who had been transported to Germany. Soon he was working with the Dutch Resistance.

Once Gert Goosens, leader of an underground group, showed Hurkos a photograph of one of the members, and asked him what he felt about the man. Hurkos said he saw him in a German uniform.

After that warning Goosens kept the man under observation, and soon had proof that he was a traitor. Before his execution he admitted that he was an agent of the Gestapo.

Peter Hurkos, like every sensitive, has a large percentage of failure. It is not the complete failures, however, but the partial successes which should serve as a warning to those who think there is a psychic answer to every problem.

A case in point is the time a psychiatrist, Dr. F. Regis Riesenman, invited Peter Hurkos to investigate the Jackson family murders in Virginia. Carroll Jackson, his wife and two daughters, disappeared in January, 1959. Their murdered bodies were not found until March, and by the time Hurkos came into the case a year later the FBI had investigated 1,475 suspects.

Dr. Riesenman and two officers of the Virginia State Police, Captain Charles M. Lindsay and Inspector Jack Hall, took Hurkos to view the Jackson home, then to the spot near Fredericksburg where the bodies of Carroll Jackson and one of his children had been found. The next day they went into Maryland where Mrs. Jackson and the other little girl had been buried in a shallow grave by the murderer.

The first day Hurkos had described a man he took to be the killer, and on the journey back from Maryland he elaborated his account. The man had two scars on his left leg, a tattoo on his arm. Then he got a picture of the house where he lived, and was able to describe his wife vividly—hair flattened with a center parting, two missing upper teeth, a pointed nose.

All this fitted one of the police suspects, except that he no longer lived at the house described. When Hurkos interviewed the man's wife, told her the number of beatings she had had from her husband and other personal secrets, she echoed the words the young arsonist had used to Hurkos years before, "I cannot lie to this man."

She then told how her husband had been away from home over the weekend of the Jackson murders, how on his return he had acted strangely, holding his head in his hands and saying, "What have I done?"

Even the husband, though he denied the murders, admitted to having had episodes of amnesia during which he might have done anything.

Although no charges could be brought against him the man was committed to the Southwestern State Hospital for the Insane by a hastily formed lunacy commission.

He was still there when the FBI arrested Melvin David Rees of Hydesville, Maryland, and charged him with the murders. Hurkos had predicted that evidence would come to light within fourteen days—and he was right. Rees was later indicted, and the first suspect quickly released from the mental hospital.

In this case Peter Hurkos was accurate with all the details of the suspect, his home and family. But he had got the wrong man. The likeliest explanation would seem to be that instead of picking up psychometric impressions from the scene he was getting telepathic impressions from the mind of one or more of the police officers. There is some evidence in support of this theory. When Hurkos began to describe the house where the man had lived—the police did not then know that he had moved—one of the officers in the car immediately recognized it as the home of a suspect. And when Hurkos described the man and his wife the same officer instantly identified them.

While Hurkos showed brilliant flashes of extrasensory perception, the case illustrates an important fact known to psychical researchers and to mediums themselves, which converts (even policemen) in their enthusiasm sometimes forget: every psychic message must be tested, and judgment suspended until proof is established.

Both Peter Hurkos and the other Dutch psychic crimebuster, Gerard Croiset, are troubled by the extraneous impressions crowding in on them which often make it difficult to differentiate the wheat from the chaff. Like most mediums they prefer to be given no more than the barest amount of information on the matter in hand, so that they can remain detached. Croiset even prefers to be consulted by telephone to eliminate outside influences as much as possible.

Such a case began when the parents of a missing boy telephoned him from a distance of ninety miles. The police had been trying to trace their son for two days without success.

Croiset told the parents not to worry. The boy was alive and well; he had taken his old bicycle and gone off in search of adventure. His idea was to reach the sea and get on a boat. He had taken the road to Valkenburg, Croiset thought, and was trying to enter Belgium. But he would be home again in a couple of days.

Despite this assurance the parents were on the phone again next day. The boy was in Belgium, Croiset said, and would reach home on Tuesday.

First thing Tuesday morning they made a third call. Croiset again assured them that their son would be home later in the day.

Just an hour later the police called to tell them that their son had been found near Dinant in Belgium. He was home before nightfall, explaining that he had cycled to the Belgian coast by the route Croiset had given them.

Croiset performed a similar feat over a far longer distance in 1960. The telephone call he received on the afternoon of December 11 was from America. The caller, Professor Walter Sandelius, a former Rhodes scholar and for many years chairman of the political science department at the University of Kansas, wanted to consult Croiset about his missing daughter.

Carol Sandelius had disappeared nearly two months before from a hospital at Topeka, where she had been a patient. Local and state police had been unable to trace her. Photographs sent to neighboring states brought reports from people who thought they had seen her in one town or another. Her father drove hundreds of miles checking, but Carol seemed to have vanished completely.

After nearly two months, by then ready to try anything, Professor Sandelius remembered having heard that law enforcement agencies sometimes got help from mediums.

Croiset told the American professor not to worry, that his

daughter was safe, and a number of facts connected with her journeying which were later found to be true. But the most important thing he said was, "You will hear something definite from your daughter in six days."

On December 17 Professor Sandelius woke early and went downstairs to the living room. There, sitting on the sofa across the room, was Carol. It was the sixth day.

Gerard Croiset appears to have a special knack of finding missing people and objects. He was sent for by the President of the District Court at Leeuwarden when documents concerning a bankruptcy case were lost.

On June 22, 1950, Croiset visited the record office of the law court. The only information he was given was that some papers were missing, and he immediately described them, saying they were in a portfolio of a certain thickness. They were still in the record office, he declared, in a room two flights up the stairs, to the left, at the rear of the building.

With the president and other court officials in tow, Croiset led the way, pointing out the room where the documents were last known to have been as he passed it, then up to the attic. There the portfolio was found, and was picked up by the president himself.

The Mayor of the Overijelse Municipality of Wierden was the principal witness in one of Croiset's most outstanding cases. A girl, aged twenty-one, had been attacked by a man who struck her two near-fatal blows on the head with a hammer. Despite her injuries the plucky young woman succeeded in wresting the weapon away from him. Her assailant then fled, leaving the hammer behind as the only clue. The hammer was even exhibited in a shop window in Wierden in a desperate hope that someone might identify the owner.

The Mayor himself contacted Croiset, who gave this description of the criminal: a tall, dark man, thirty to thirty-five years old, with a deformed left ear, who wears a ring with a blue stone. The hammer was not his property, but belonged to a man of fifty-five, who lives in one of three cottages with low sheds standing near each other. Behind his house was an old-fashioned rainbutt.

This remarkably detailed picture brought back the attention of the police to a man who had been one of several casual suspects, though there had been nothing to justify even a formal interrogation, let alone an arrest. They still failed to find evidence on which to charge him. But a few months later the man was arrested for an offense against public morals. After his trial on this charge he confessed to the attack on the girl.

Every fact Croiset had given connected with the criminal and the neighbor from whom he borrowed the hammer was proved correct, except that the police could not verify his ownership of a ring with a blue stone.

Croiset's powers have been investigated, and many of his cases analyzed, by Professor W. H. C. Tenhaeff, Director of the Parapsychology Institute at the University of Utrecht. When Croiset has been called in to assist the police, consultations have usually taken place with Professor Tenhaeff present.

Like all sensitives, Croiset has his failures, and cases which offer good evidence from a psychical research point of view are often unsatisfactory from the police angle. In the opinion of Professor Tenhaeff some of the failures result from Croiset having identified too closely with the subject. Many sensitives, he believes, tend to trace events in the lives of others which are similar to what they have experienced themselves.

One case which illustrates this sound theory arose when an acquaintance of Professor Tenhaeff consulted Croiset because he suspected that two members of his staff were involved in gin smuggling. When he was shown a photograph of the staff, Croiset immediately picked out the two men from the several dozen people in the group and said they were the thieves.

But then, instead of producing more helpful information about their smuggling activities, his interest switched completely to a third man in the group. This man, Croiset alleged, had swindled a war orphan whose money was in his control. Furthermore, his employer—the man Croiset was addressing—had in his possession a notebook which belonged to the defaulting guardian, and in it was evidence of the fraud.

The man admitted that he had the notebook.

The point of interest is that Gerard Croiset himself had a miserable time when he was looked after by foster-parents. So he could easily identify with a wronged orphan, and to him the dishonest guardian was a greater villain than the gin smugglers. Most of us would agree.

All the same, when I next went to Holland after hearing this, the temptation to slip something past Customs was markedly less than on previous trips.

□

CHAPTER THIRTEEN

From the Murderer's Viewpoint

> When we goes up to London Town,
> We likes to drown ahr sorrers;
> We likes to go to the waxwork show,
> And sit in the Chamber of 'Orrers.
> There's a luvly image of Mother there,
> And we do enjoy it rather:
> We likes to see her 'ow she was,
> The night she strangled Father

I quote this old music-hall verse to illustrate, as it aptly does, that there are unexpected ways of looking at things, even murder. And because, for some no doubt traumatic reason, I rather relish the rhyme myself. So, incidentally, did that least morbid of men, G. K. Chesterton.

Old Mrs. Palmer, too, had a distinctly personal viewpoint. Long after the sudden ceremonial demise of her son, William, the happy-go-luckiest of poisoners, she was wont to murmur in a tone of marked reproach, "They hanged my saintly Billy." She stuck to the belief that of her seven children William was, in her own words, "the best of the lot."

Mothers are privileged to make their own judgments. When Mrs. W. F. Floyd was told of the death of her son her comment was, "Charles was a good boy." Charles, better known as "Pretty

Boy" Floyd, had achieved his ambition of becoming America's Public Enemy No. 1, before being shot down by the FBI.

Morally—and that is the right word—everyone has a right to his opinion, even the murderer; though a mind directed to murder will not admit the rights of others. Single-minded selfishness of outlook is—indeed, has to be—the killer's common trait. It is what makes a murderer tick, or if not necessarily the mainspring, is an essential part of his mechanism.

This does not prevent him from being a man of faith and hope, if not of charity. The entire Szenzi family of Vienna died after eating mushrooms cultivated in their own cellar. The gardener, Frensci, accused of multiple murder, admitted having planted poisonous fungi among the mushrooms. He had wanted to stop his daughter from marrying a nephew of the house. The daughter, in service with the Szenzi family, had eaten of their meal and had died. Asked whether he had considered this danger, Frensci replied, "My daughter had a pure heart. I believed the poison could not harm her."

A pitiable and moronic faith, we might think. Less confident in matters of theology was Jonathan Wild, the notorious London thief who, as an organizer of crime, graft and corruption, could have given useful hints to the modern Mafia. Before his execution Wild inquired the meaning of the text, "Cursed is everyone that hangeth on a tree." He also wished to be told the state of the soul immediately after its departure from the body.

His confessors evidently did not know the answers. The *Newgate Calendar* records: "He was advised to direct his attention to *matters of more importance,* and sincerely to repent of the crimes he had committed." The italics are mine; like Wild, I am left wondering what could be of more importance to him at that stage of his career.

Jean Videle, who killed a constable in Sydney, Australia, and attempted to burn the body, had more consideration given to his last wishes. Public executions were then still in vogue, and Videle invited the entire crowd, numbering several thousands, to pray for him before he was hanged. All knelt.

In contrast with Jonathan Wild's uncertainties about his condition in the next life, a touching belief was exhibited only last year by an African woman. In Johannesburg, Elizabeth Radebe, found guilty of murdering another woman, was let off with the comparatively light sentence of eight years' imprisonment. Mrs. Radebe protested strongly—she wanted to be hanged instead. Not because she thought she deserved it. She insisted that she had had no quarrel with the other lady, and had not killed her, but explained, "I want to go meet the deceased so we can discuss the matter." The judge was unable to grant her request.

Faith not only in an afterlife, but in his ability to return and communicate, seems to have been held by Nathan Leopold, of the Leopold-Loeb duo which set out to prove that murder can be fun. Expecting he would draw the death penalty, Leopold proffered an egocentric plan for the world's ten most puzzling riddles to be sealed in his tomb, and a national committee of scientists elected to hold séances. For his part he would endeavor—from the "astral plane," where apparently he assumed he would be situated—to make contact and provide answers to the riddles.

The opportunity never arose. Leopold was sentenced to life imprisonment; the judge meant "life" to be taken literally, for he expressed a hope that neither of the homicidal students would ever be released. Despite this harsh (if understandable in the context of the crime) rider to the sentence, Leopold was paroled in 1958, having served thirty-four years. In fairness to him, and intending no cynical boost for the prison system of reform, it should be mentioned that he was said to be a much changed personality.

We cannot be certain whether a death wish motivated Neville Heath, who in 1946 killed and mutilated Margery Gardner at a Notting Hill hotel. Certainly he made no great effort to escape the death penalty. Heath's sexual relations appear to have been normal at most times. Just a few nights before the murder, Yvonne Marie Symonds, a 19-year-old girl who expected to marry Heath, had slept with him in the bed on which Margery Gardner died. His meeting with Margery Gardner, a known masochist, may have unleashed Heath's latent sadism. Then within a week of the first killing Heath murdered Doreen Marshall, a girl he met at Bournemouth, exhibiting the same sort of savagery.

It has been suggested that Heath's second murder was done in a deliberate attempt to strengthen the ground for a plea of insanity. More persuasive, I think, is the theory that he could no longer hold himself in check. His counsel, Mr. J. D. Casswell, Q.C., recalls that at their first meeting Heath wanted to plead guilty to the indictment. He changed his mind, but after the verdict became one of the very few murderers to refuse to appeal against conviction.

Before the execution he wrote a letter to his younger brother. An ex-R.A.F. flyer, Heath very typically employed the jocular tone and phraseology of his decade, but he twice suggests the idea of spirit return. ". . . I won't be seeing you again but perhaps in the days to come you'll feel a friendly Gremlin ease your aircraft out of a sticky position. You may recognise the touch." (His brother was about to join the Royal Air Force.) And again later . . . "Get your 'A' licence and go ahead. You can do great things. . . . Don't you bloody well let me down or I'll haunt you, and I have a feeling I can be a most unpleasant ghost."

How much real belief he was expressing is a matter of doubt, but context and circumstance argue more than just a manner of speaking.

One murderer adhered to the basic tenets of Spiritualism in his outlook. It was through his landlady, Mrs. Sykes, who claimed to be a medium, that Patrick Power became greatly interested in spirit communication. And she was the woman he murdered.

Motive here is a mystery. Power, an ex-soldier, was a heavy drinker, and occasionally suffered attacks of malaria, a legacy from his service abroad. He was drunk the day Mrs. Sykes, coming home from shopping, reminded him that he owed her rent. Then, according to Power, "I remember nothing more after that until I saw Mrs. Sykes' body on the floor and me standing over it. I don't know what happened at all."

This defense is a bit threadworn, but the fact that it can be true is what has made it popular. In Power's case his record made it reasonable to give him the benefit of the doubt. He did not get it; he was hanged.

What did happen was that Power attacked Mrs. Sykes in maniacal fashion with a hammer and a breadknife. Yet he had always been on very good terms with her. The hangman, William Willis, who executed more than a hundred condemned murderers, was impressed by Power as "the most powerful man I have ever seen; a tower of strength." But Power had never been known to use his great strength to bully anyone. Drunk or sober, he was never quarrelsome, but always easygoing and pleasant. Why then did he attack Mrs. Sykes with deadly weapons when he could have broken her without effort with his bare hands?

Patrick Power refused to appeal. In his Spiritualist convictions he appears to have been deeply sincere. At the very end he joked that he would come back after his execution to collect the few cigarettes he had left unsmoked; then walked to the gallows with a smile on his lips, secure in the faith that his life would continue in another sphere.

If Patrick Power did return, either for his cigarettes or other purposes, it is not on record.

An unusual story of communication centers around Robinson, the Charing Cross Trunk murderer. Robert Goldsbrough, the industrialist who took Ernest Bevin, British Foreign Secretary, to séances during the war,* told me of this experience.

Goldsbrough and some friends were holding a séance in a small room in Rochester Row, Victoria, when an unexpected intruder took control of the medium.

"I know I am dead," said the voice. "I can still feel the rope around my neck. But I can't get away from her eyes. They keep staring at me."

He sounded agitated, but when spoken to soothingly he calmed down a little. He said he was Robinson. He was haunted by remorse, but nonetheless he protested that he had been innocent of willful murder. The victim was attempting to blackmail him, they quarreled and he pushed her. In falling she struck her head on the fender. When she failed to get up he bent to help her, only to realize that she was dead.

It had happened next door to the room where the séance was being held. Rochester Row police station was just across the street. But instead of going to the police the terror-stricken Robinson had dismembered and then tried to dispose of the body.

Three days after this Goldsbrough chanced to meet his friend, Detective Sergeant Handyside, who assisted Superintendent

---

* See *Exploring the Psychic World.*

Cornish on the Charing Cross Trunk Murder and other cases. He told him about the séance.

The Scotland Yard man's reaction was much stronger than Goldsbrough had expected.

"My God!" he exclaimed. "I thought I was the only man alive who knew that."

Handyside explained why he was so astounded. When Robinson, after being sentenced, was taken down to the cells underneath the Old Bailey, Handyside went to see him.

The man he had arrested reiterated once again that he was not a murderer. Yet, he said, he was looking forward to his execution, *because the eyes of the dead woman were constantly staring at him.*

No one else knew of that so far as Handyside had been aware.

Robinson also tried to convince Handyside that the victim's death was an accident, even after the jury had rejected his version of what happened. Juries are always reluctant to accept any other explanation than murder when death is followed by dismemberment; Robinson lost any chance he might have had of evading the death sentence when he started butchering. Yet Handyside, the experienced Scotland Yard detective, confessed that after that last grim interview, seeing the man haunted by such fears, he half believed his story.

André Chenier, the guillotined French poet, was more interested in his art than his innocence. At one of Victor Hugo's table séances—the famous writer had a keen interest in spirit communication—he is said to have completed a poem left unfinished at the time of his beheading.

Not a few people with one foot over the threshold of death have, so to speak, stepped back and afterward have given some account of it. Only one convicted murderer has had this opportunity, so far as I recall. Bearing the very ordinary name John Smith his celebrity earned him the much more distinctive nickname "Half-hanged" Smith.

Smith was carted to Tyburn (near where Marble Arch now stands) on Christmas Eve of 1705. There he was—as the *Newgate Calendar*'s euphemistic phrase has it—"turned off in the usual manner."

The long drop had not then been invented. Hanging was a

matter of slow strangulation. If drawing and quartering were part of the punishment, the victim usually lived to experience the full horror.

John Smith was dangling from the scaffold when, dramatically, a messenger brought his reprieve. By the time they cut him down he had been suspended for fifteen minutes. When he had somewhat recovered he was invited to describe his sensations during what he thought were his last moments. He replied that he had been sensible of great pain, occasioned by the weight of his body. And then he felt his spirit in a strange commotion, violently pressing upward.

Those who favor hanging as a warning not to go and murder likewise, may be discouraged to learn that it had no such salutary lesson on the man who had already experienced the worst of it. John Smith was arraigned twice more for capital crimes. One charge he emerged from safely when, the jury having brought in an inconclusive verdict, the issue was left to a panel of judges, who found in his favor. The other he escaped owing to the convenient death of the chief witness for the prosecution.

"Half-hanged" Smith, who felt his spirit rising on the scaffold, was undoubtedly a lucky man. High authority halted his execution in the nick of time. One or two lucky men have been saved by what many believed to be intervention by the Highest Authority. John Lee, for example, became known as "The Man They Could Not Hang," when the gallows trap three times failed to operate.

Lee committed a particularly despicable murder, slaying his benefactress, Mrs. Emma Keyse, then setting her house on fire in an attempt to cover up the crime.

The condemned man ate a hearty breakfast, as they used to say—encouraging the comfortable idea that the sensible prisoner took his hanging sportingly, attending the event with a tranquil mind in a well-nourished body. Lee did, in fact, order chicken with vegetables, muffins, cakes and tea, before keeping his appointment with hangman James Berry.

When all was ready Berry pressed the lever. The trap failed to operate. Lee was removed and the trap tested without his weight. It worked perfectly. So they had another try at execution. Again the trap failed . . . and then again.

After the third unsuccessful effort to hang Lee the prison chaplain was in a state of nervous prostration, the prison surgeon was begging that the farce should be stopped. The governor consulted the Under-Sheriff, and the hanging was called off.

John Lee later had his sentence commuted to life imprisonment. When he was released, after serving twenty-one years, the former sinner became a publican.

The official explanation of what had occurred blamed two days of continuous rain for having soaked the planks, causing the wood to swell. The pressure of Lee's weight, the theory ran, then jointed the timbers together; his removal released the pressure and allowed the trap to function. While this seems to me an unlikely story, I am even less inclined to accept the explanation of supernormal intervention, which a large section of the public came to believe. The appropriate comment on administrative inefficiency was made by a local resident in a letter to the *Times:*

"It appears that John Lee, who broke the skull and cut the throat of his benefactress, and then set fire to her body, is not to be hanged as, owing to the rain on Sunday night, the drop did not work easily the next morning. It should be announced that in future, executions will take place 'weather permitting.'"

James Berry, who admittedly had his own reputation to think of and may have been reluctant to support the swollen plank theory, later contributed a story. Before the fiasco, while he was inspecting the execution shed, a warder said to him:

"I heard Lee laugh and asked what it meant. He told my mate, 'You'll never hang me.' My mate asked why, and Lee said, 'Just wait and see.'"

This threw no light at all on why the trap did not work; but maybe Lee did have a presentiment that it would fail.

John Lee was guilty beyond all reasonable doubt. Joseph Samuels was innocent, and better merited the overtime his guardian angel must have put in, if that is where credit for his amazing escape should be allowed.

Standing under the gallows, Samuels, without excitement or rancor, proclaimed his innocence and accused Isaac Simmonds of the crime for which he had been condemned.

Simmonds was suspected of being an accomplice. The police

had forced him to witness the execution—this was at Sydney, Australia, in the days of public hangings.

When Samuels accused him Simmonds shouted back denials. The calm demeanor of Samuels so contrasted with Simmonds' nervous bluster that everyone in the crowd believed the man under the noose. They pushed forward, calling for his release.

Fearing a rescue and a lynching the Provost Marshal signaled the driver of the execution cart, who lashed his horses. They lunged forward, leaving Samuels dancing on air. For just a second—then the rope parted and Samuels fell to the cobbles, shaken but alive.

The military guard hastily formed a square of bayonets to hold back the crowd. Samuels was put back on the cart. The executioner fixed a new rope. Again the horses were whipped into motion, and the prisoner swung in mid-air.

The rope did not break. This time it unwove, strand by strand, until Samuels' feet touched the ground.

One contemporary account states that despite the clamor for Samuels' release—"It is the hand of God!" they cried—a third attempt was made to hang him. Dazed and inert, he had to be supported by soldiers while a third rope was made ready. Although his body was allowed to swing much less violently than before, again the rope snapped, close to his neck.

Even the Provost Marshal had had enough. He stayed the execution and went to report to the Governor. Samuels was granted a reprieve.

Tests of the third rope showed that the only flaw was where it had broken. Weights to a total of 392 pounds were hung from it. After one of the strands had been deliberately cut through, and then a second, the third and remaining strand continued to support the full weight without breaking.

Evidence was procured which brought about the release of Samuels and the conviction of Isaac Simmonds. Apparently Simmonds was hanged without incident. Both men were confirmed criminals, and if a hand reached out to save Samuels it did not guide him to reform. He was last seen at sea, with a storm blowing up, in a boat he had stolen to escape pursuit by the police for another crime.

Sometimes murderers have blamed obsessing spirits for their crimes, not always very convincingly. Victor Terry, who held up a bank at Worthing, killing a bank guard in the process, claimed that his mind was possessed by the spirit of Jack "Legs" Diamond.

Terry, a product of his times, once stated his philosophy, "When I was a kid they told me I would hang one day. But what does it matter? If the noose don't get you the H-bomb will."

At his trial Terry put forward a defense of diminished responsibility. Dr. Arthur Spencer Paterson, head of the psychiatric department at the West London Hospital, testified that he had considered the possibility that Terry might be shamming, but had concluded otherwise.

"When I get the feeling to do harm it is not me," Terry had told the psychiatrist. "I think my mind was an offspring of one of the big gangsters in America. I believe that when a person dies, his mind or spirit leaves him and goes into another body, and one of these minds has gone into my body. If someone speaks to me roughly, one minute I am normal and the next I am like a blooming monster."

Dr. Paterson asked him, "Does the real you ever talk to Legs Diamond?"

"Yes, often," Terry replied. "He does not talk to me out loud. I hear the words like when I am reading a book."

In Dr. Paterson's judgment Terry remembered his actions only as if committed in a dream over which he had no control. "He is living in a gangster world. . . . He thought he was this man Diamond and signed his name Diamond."

Prosecuting counsel, referring to Terry's flight through the length of England and into Scotland with his "gun moll," asked: "When he decided to abandon the tour of Devon and Cornwall by taxi, to buy a gun in Salisbury, return to London and then get the train to Scotland, was that on orders, suggestions or recommendations from Mr. Diamond?"

"Some of it was," said the psychiatrist.

Terry, a Purple Heart eater, had been taking five times the normal dosage. Mr. Justice Stable ruled out the defense plea that the mind of the accused was so diseased from taking drugs as to bring him within the rules of diminished responsibility.

Victor Terry, who said that when he was normal he could not think why he wanted to be a great gangster, but had known he was doomed and would hang in 1961, was found guilty of murder and sentenced to death in March of that year.

There was nothing tentative about Marten, the French murderer and train-robbing Robin Hood (he said he was taking from the rich to give to the poor). He had an astonishing run of success before the Sûreté Nationale caught up with him in 1954.

"I was only performing a task as ordered by the astral spirits," Marten then excused himself at his trial. "No one is a master of his own destiny." His wife, an accomplice in his crimes as well as his séances, had kept a minutely detailed diary of their activities.

This was an honest belief in communication directed to dishonest ends. Something more grotesque emerges in an anecdote told by the poet Henry Wadsworth Longfellow, which casts eerie light on Boston's most notorious murder.

The case became a *cause célèbre* due largely to the eminence of the principals. The victim was Dr. George Parkman, leading citizen and philanthropist, donor of the Parkman Chair of Anatomy (at one time held by Oliver Wendell Holmes), and uncle of the historian, Francis Parkman. The murderer was Professor Webster, who occupied the chair of chemistry at Harvard, the only incumbent—to the best of my knowledge—to bestow academic tone upon the death cell.

Longfellow was present at a dinner given by Professor Webster some time prior to the murder. After the meal the Professor put on an entertainment for his guests which, even by nineteenth century Boston standards one would suppose, must have been considered an *outré* performance.

Lights were lowered. A servant carried in a bowl of blazing chemicals, which cast a horrible green luminescence round the room. Webster produced a rope with a noose at one end. He put the noose around his neck, and threw the loose end of the rope over the chandelier.

Then he leaned over the flame flickering in the bowl, his head tilted, his tongue protruding, giving a ghastly impression of a man who had been hanged.

Webster's motive for this bit of Grand Guignol remains a mystery. Consciously or otherwise he produced a macabre simulation of future reality.

A sadder premonition came true on the first day of January, 1961, in New York. It happened to be a Sunday.

In the Bar Puerto Rico, a beer joint, sat Angel Rafael Ortega, an unemployed factory worker. A man burst into the room—Incarnation Martinez.

"I don't have long to live," he yelled. "I want someone to kill me tonight."

Martinez cried the same words over and over, till someone punched him in the face to stop the noise. He staggered out into the street.

Angel Ortega followed him.

Seconds later everyone in the bar heard a loud scream. When they rushed out Incarnation Martinez was slumped on the pavement. Dead.

Angel Ortega had vanished.

In Ortega's room nearby his girl friend was waiting. "I just killed a guy," he said when he came in. "And I don't even know him."

The police came for him a few minutes later. "For the last two months," Ortega told them, "I've walked the streets at night with my knife, waiting for something to happen. Tonight I met someone who needed me."

There is a theory that murderers and murderees are predestined to meet. Nowhere does it find better support than in this case of the two so-ironically named Puerto Ricans, an Incarnation terminated by an Angel of death.

Were the "Brides in the Bath" predestined to meet Mr. George Joseph Smith? Only, perhaps, insofar as they were lonely, unwanted women, ripe for victimization. Dozens of others would have suited Smith, and a kindlier fate would have delivered the "brides" into more scrupulous hands. But there again . . . fate.

George Joseph Smith was the most mundane of murderers, lacking in both imagination and ambition. Not the man to benefit from a psychic warning.

This story involves three rather shattering coincidences . . . unless we prefer to bring that ol' devil destiny back into the picture.

The least remarkable is that the playwright and criminologist, F. Tennyson Jesse, a great-niece of the poet, should have been acquainted with one of Smith's victims, Bessie Mundy. On one occasion when they met, Mundy told Miss Jesse that her husband, Henry Williams, had left her after borrowing her savings.

The second coincidence was a chance meeting in a Bristol street of Bessie Mundy and her runaway husband, Smith, alias Henry Williams. This resulted in a reconciliation—Miss Mundy owned property he had yet to obtain. Her subsequent drowning was the first in Smith's murder series.

The strangest coincidence was when Miss Jesse, visiting a fortune-teller at Worthing, bumped into a man who was on his way out. He was a stranger; but something about him arrested her attention sufficiently for her to mention him to the fortune-teller.

Mr. Omega had just read the man's palm. His life, he had perceived, would have a sudden and unfortunate termination.

When F. Tennyson Jesse saw the same man again a year later he was standing in the dock, accused of the murder of her friend, Bessie Mundy.

The life of George Joseph Smith was very soon due to come to its "sudden and unfortunate termination"—at the end of a rope.

CHAPTER FOURTEEN

□

The Psychic Eye of Justice

TRADITIONALLY, Justice is a lady who wears an eye bandage. This could be because she is too sensitive to stand the sight of so much injustice in the world which, we must charitably assume, she is powerless to prevent. At times, however, the handicapped lady gives indications of possessing an eye which can penetrate the blindfold—a psychic eye.

Elliott O'Donnell, a famous collector of ghost tales, told one such intriguing story. A bank manager, while visiting Bath for the first time, one night had a dream. He was with a young man, handsome had it not been for a vivid red scar on one cheek, and they were talking about the city. The young man said he was a former resident, and he suggested that his companion should go to the Circus (a well-known street in Bath) at seven o'clock the next night. This request was repeated before the dreamer awoke.

The following day, having been unable to dismiss the dream from his mind, the bank manager went to the Circus at the appointed time. It was a fine night, but freezing. The only person in sight was a middle-aged man who, walking towards him, slipped on a patch of ice and fell. The bank manager, helping him to his feet, had a fleeting thought that there was something familiar about the man's features, though he could not remember having met him before.

The stranger, unhurt but badly shaken, said he was on his way to the railway station to catch the 7:30 train to London. His hotel being near the station, the bank manager offered to walk with him. He learned that his companion, having returned to Bath after a long absence, had found that all his friends were dead or gone away, and he would be relieved to get back to London.

The dream still on his mind, the bank manager worried about not having waited at the Circus. He even went there the next night at the same time to see if anything would happen. Nothing did, and he decided to forget the whole thing. But he noted the dream in his diary.

Although the dream never recurred, for a whole year the young man with the red scar often came into his thoughts. Then one day he had to go to a London police court to give evidence in a case involving his bank. When he entered the court a charge of burglary with violence was being tried. He at once recognized the man in the dock—it was the middle-aged traveler he had assisted at the Circus.

Two witnesses gave evidence that the man had broken into their house and assaulted them. The prisoner pleaded that at the time of the crime he was in Bath. Unfortunately, he had no means of proving it.

Then the bank manager stepped forward. The day and hour in question coincided with the meeting he well remembered. Thanks to the complete alibi he was able to provide, the accused man was acquitted.

When told about the vital dream afterwards the man produced a photograph of his son who, he explained, had had a red scar on his face resulting from a railway accident. It was the young man of the dream, whom the bank manager still vividly remembered. He had died in Bath, the father said, ten years before.

There can be little doubt that this remarkable intervention saved an innocent man from being found guilty. Here the psychic eye of justice was wide open. But such instances are rare.

Conversely, mistakes on the part of the courts occur more often than we like to imagine, despite the vaunted high standards of the British legal system. Those who believe the American system to be more reliable need not tax themselves delving through dusty legal tomes to be disillusioned. They need only read

The Court of Last Resort, a far from fictional work by the most popular of crime writers, Erle Stanley Gardner.

Then there is the other side of the picture: criminals who flaunt justice for lack of evidence to convict them. Crime rates are rising in most countries. Serious and violent crimes committed in the United States in 1967 totaled 3.8 million, a 16.5 percent increase over 1966. There was a murder, rape or assault to kill every minute.

So whichever way we look at it, every available aid to prevent or combat crime needs to be utilized.

The doubtful reader may be wondering whether I am about to recommend that mediums should take over from the police. Edgar Wallace, I think, once suggested that mediums should be employed at Scotland Yard. And, after all, there are quite a number of cases in which the police were admittedly baffled, and might have stayed that way, if the psychic world had not provided a lead. Nevertheless, to my knowledge, the psychic world is not crammed with crime-solving Perry Masons and Sherlock Holmeses waiting to be unleashed.

What one might reasonably recommend is that psychic communications reaching the police should be carefully sifted. Some police departments do this conscientiously enough already. Others lump them together with all the crank reports that every major investigation will attract. Some rightly fall in this category, but that is no reason for dismissing the rest.

Whether to take the initiative and consult sensitives is a larger question. Perhaps they could help by providing shortcuts which could save a lot of investigative work in blind alleys. At times they would provide a key to the full solution of a crime. So it should pay any police department to be in touch with one or two people with psychic ability, who can be asked to help when normal procedure is making no headway.

If they were to be employed on a regular basis or consulted as a matter of routine, then I am more skeptical of what results might be forthcoming—though I wish some police department would be bold enough to try it, for it would be a most interesting experiment.

Certainly a high percentage of success should not be expected. I have sat at a good many séances where criminals or, more often, their victims have purported to communicate. Sometimes the results have been dramatic, and intriguing to the psychical researcher or the psychologist. Very few have provided information which could be of value to the police.

In all of this there are dangers to guard against—an obvious one being that after a few successes officers might place too much confidence in a sensitive, and in accepting his ideas neglect other lines of inquiry. Or the medium might be influenced unknowingly by their ideas, and throw them back at them with the stamp of supernormal authority.

A bare statement by a medium, "John Doe is guilty" or "Richard Roe is innocent," has no more weight than the opinion of any other citizen. His function is to supply a fact, a clue he has not received from normal sources, which can then be substantiated by investigation. What the medium believes is not evidence. John Doe has to be *proved* guilty beyond reasonable doubt. If we remember that, then extrasensory perception can be useful.

This book has laid no claim to high moral tone. So at this late stage let me recall two stories with a lesson for us all.

Some years ago the Institute of Literature of the Chinese Academy of Science in Peking published a book, *Stories of Not Being Afraid of Ghosts*. In a moralizing introduction it was stated: "This book includes thirty-five stories about not being afraid of ghosts. They show the courage of Chinese people in ancient times who dared to defy ghosts. *Today everyone knows there are no such things as ghosts.* But while there are no demons like those described in these tales there are many things which resemble them—imperialism, reactionaries, difficulties and obstacles in work." (My italics—F.A.)

What then were they courageously defying? Ghosts do not exist, so it was necessary for Chairman Mao to invent substitutes!

More years ago Joshua Coppersmith was arrested in New York for "attempting to extort funds from ignorant and superstitious people by exhibiting a device which he says will convey the human voice any distance over metallic wires so that it will be heard by the listener at the other end." A Boston newspaper seized the opportunity to pontificate: "*Well-informed people know that it is impossible to transmit the human voice over wires* as may be done with dots and dashes and signals of the Morse code, *and that were it possible to do so, the thing would be of no practical value.* The authorities who apprehended this criminal are to be congratulated, and it is to be hoped that his punishment will be prompt and fitting. . . ." (My italics—F.A.)

Then whatever became of those carrier pigeons? Are you receiving, Alexander Graham Bell?

Ghosts have been known to all races since the dawn of man's history. There are those, such as Chairman Mao, who would deny that they have ever appeared.

So much for minds closed to the past.

Every new discovery, such as the telephone, has been derided by the unimaginative. To ignorantly condemn things as being of no practical value has usually been thought of as a clinching argument.

So much for minds closed to the future.

Today even the governments of America and Russia are taking extrasensory perception seriously enough to experiment with a view to its possible usefulness in war and espionage. If psychic abilities can conceivably be employed for such purposes then why not in the battle against crime, which every country is perpetually waging?

Psychic perception may one day play a fully recognized part in crime prevention and solution. Sooner or later it must be properly tried. Better soon than late.

INDEX

Abbott, Inspector, 52
Abel, 5
Aken, Colin, 31–32
Aken, Graham, 32
Aken, Myrna Joy, 31–32
Alexander, King (Serbia), 78
Alexander, Lord Chief Baron, 90
Allaway, Thomas Henry, 76
Ameer Ben Ali, 12
Ames, Flora, 78–79
Anderson, Andy, 42–46
Avory, Sir Horace, 75–76

Bailey, Lilian, 141–42
Barbier-Morin, Mme., 34–35
Barnes, Chief Constable, 27
Barroso, Ary, 144
Baxter, Wynne, 20
Beckwith, Fred C., 16
Bell, John C., 64, 65–66
Bell, Mrs. John C., 64, 65–66
Bellingham, John, 79
Bennett, Paul, 141
Benson, Archbishop, 15
Berry, James, 172–73
Bevin, Ernest, 170
Binet, Madame, 33–34
Black Hawk, 128
Blackwood, Algernon, 107, 108
Blackwood, Sir Arthur, 108
Blower, Derek, 28
Blower, Mrs. Flora, 28–29
Blower, William, 28–29
Bond, Frederick Bligh, 144

Bonneville, Captain, 129
Booher, Fred, 39, 42
Booher, Henry, 39, 40
Booher, Mrs. Henry, 39, 42
Booher, Vernon, 39–42
Booth, William, 12
Bournemouth, England, 75–76
"Brides in the Bath," 177
Brighton Trunk Crime No. 1, 29–31
Brown, Fred Gordon, 20
Brutus, 78
Burchell, Mrs., 78
Burke (murderer), 49

Caesar, Julius, 78
Cain, 5
Calpurnia, 78
Camb, James, 31
Camberg, Aard, 159
Cammaert, Police Captain, 157
Carey, Constable, 36–37
Carlin, Francis, 49–54
Cassius, 78
Casswell, J. D., 169
Catlin, George, 129
Caunt, James, 143
Chapman, Annie, 20
Charing Cross Trunk Murder, 170–71
Chenier, André, 171
Chesterton, G. K., 21, 77, 166
Chilwell, Nottinghamshire, England, 69

Chimes (psychic journal), 58
Christie, 11
Churchill, Winston, 82
Cicero, 59
Clifton, Margaret, 126–27
Clynes, J. R., 121–22
Columbus, Christopher, 129
Comstock, Archie, 86
Coppersmith, Joshua, 182
Corder, William, 47–49, 90
Cordovil, Herve, 144
Cortini, Alfredo, 116–20
Court of Last Resort, The (Gardner), 181
Cox, Detective Inspector, 55
Cream, Neill, 13
Croiset, Gerard, 157, 162–65
Cromby, Gabriel, 39, 42
Crookes, Sir William, 67
Cummins, Geraldine, 144

D.H.B., 88–89
Dallas, Miss, 139
Dalton, Bill, 133
Dawson, Warrington, 33
Dearden, Harold, 22
Decker, Frank, 112
Deeming, Frederick Bailey, 13
Delbeck-Dupont, M., 158–59
Dennis, Eugenie, 29–30
Dhingra, Madar Lal, 151–52
Diamond, Jack "Legs," 175
Disraeli, Benjamin, 13
Doran, Joe, 85–87
Dowding, Lord, 103, 105, 106
Doyle, Sir Arthur Conan, 138
Doyle, Denis Conan, 138
Draga, Queen (Serbia), 78–79
Duesler, William, 63–66
Dunne, J. W., 58
Durant, James, 87
Durban Castle (liner), 31
Durnez, Gerard, 158
Durnez, Lucien, 158–59
Dyer, Ernest, 50–54
Dyer, Mrs. Ernest, 53–54

Eastbourne, England, 73–74
Eastman, Charles A., 130
Eddowes, Catherine, 20
Electro-convulsion therapy, 103
Ellington, Percy, 28
Enright, Chief Commissioner, 29
Evans, Britton, 96
Evans, Franklin B., 94
Eve, Justice, 144
Experiment with Time, An (Dunne), 58

Faurot, Commissioner, 29
Federal Bureau of Investigation, 160, 167
Feller, George, 131–33
Feller, Kathy, 131–33
Field, Alfred, 74–75
Flammarion, Camille, 93
Floyd, Charles "Pretty Boy," 166–67
Floyd, Mrs. W. F., 166
Foster, Stephen, 77
Fox family, 61–68
Frazer, Kenneth, 71, 72
Freiderich, Roberta, 58
Frensci (murderer), 167

Galemont, Robert, 81
Garden of Eden, 5
Gardner, Erle Stanley, 181
Gardner, Margery, 168
Gardstein (murderer), 84
Garrett, Eileen, 104
Ghan, Tran van, 59
Gibbons, James, 15
Gibson, Gay, 31
Gier, Mike, 39–42
Gladstone, Professor, 37–38
Gladstone, William, 13
Gladu, Moise, 43
Glaister, John, 87
Goldsbrough, Robert, 170–71
Gony family, 81–82
Goosens, Gert, 160
Grant, Murdoch, 70–72
Grant, Robert, 71

Gray, Martha, 133
Gray, Sally, 133–36
Gray, Thomas, 74–75
Greeley, Horace, 67
Gregory, John, 138–39
Gregory, Mrs. John, 138–39
Groebel, Miss, 74

Hall, Jack, 160
Handyside, Detective Sergeant, 170–71
Harrison, Doris, 54–55
Harrison, Frank, 54–55
Hawke, Anthony, 142
Hayward, Edward, 44–46
Hayward, George, 45–46
Heaslip, Dr., 39
Heath, Neville, 168–69
Hicks, Sir Seymour, 80
Higgins, Erma, 42
Hillier, Constable, 29–30
Hitler, Adolf, 19
Hoffman, Mrs. Myrtle, 85–87
Hollister, Bessie, 100
Holmes, Oliver Wendell, 176
Hornsby, Reuben, 123–27
Hornsby, Sarah, 123–27
Hughes, Bert, 54–55
Hughes, Myrtle, 54–55
Hugo, Victor, 171
Hume, David, 91
Hummel, Abe, 96–97
Hurkos, Peter, 156–62
Hyde, William H., 68

Ihland case, 133–36
Indians, American, 124–31
Isaac, 5
Ivens, Richard, 100–1

Jack the Ripper, 11–23, 24
Jackson family, 160–61
James, Henry, 33
James, John, 129
James, William, 6, 33, 100, 106
Jansen family, 157
Jencken, Samuel, 67

Jerome, District Attorney, 98
Jesse, F. Tennyson, 178
Jesus Christ, 104
Johnson, Mrs. E., 140–43
Jones, Mrs. Ann, 28
Jonson, Mr., 112–15

Kane, Elisha, 67
Keats, John, 128
Kelly, Jack, 24–25
Keyse, Mrs. Emma, 172
King, Charlie, 43–46
Klaus, Annie, 150–51
Kuerten, Peter, 11, 94–95, 100–1

Lalcacca, Cawas, 152
Lalemant, Jerome, 130
Landru, 11
Lane (actor), 80
Langsner, Maximilien, 38–42
Leaf, Horace, 112, 114
Leary, Mrs. Alec, 143
Ledru, Robert, 154–55
Lee, John, 172–73
Lees, Claude, 18
Lees, Eva, 18
Lees, Robert James, 13–22
Legg, Mrs. Jane, 28–29
Leopold, Nathan, 168
Leslie, Detective, 40–41
Leslie, Sir Shane, 92
Lightfoot, Ben, 136
Lindsay, Charles M., 160
Liston, Fred, 153
Lodge, Sir Oliver, 108, 120
Lombardo, Roberto, 115–20
Longacre, Inspector, 40
Longfellow, Henry Wadsworth, 176
Losey, Amelia, 66
Lowe, Constable, 44
Lynd, Robert, 108–9

Mackenzie, John, 70
McLauchlan, Scotty, 36–38
McLaughlan, "Mac," 151–52
MacLeod, Hugh, 70–72

Macy, Walter J., 85–86
Mallery, Garrick, 129
Malloy, James F., 86–87
"Man They Could Not Hang, The," 172
Manning, Henry Edward, 15
Mao, Chairman, 183
Marcoz, Mme., 34–35
Marjan, Ali, 56
Marshall, Doreen, 168
Marten (murderer), 176
Marten, Maria, 47–49, 90
Martin, Stuart, 29
Martinez, Incarnation, 177
Mason, Blake, 86
Mathers, James, 133–36
Maude, Justice, 90
Mercer, Chief Inspector, 74
Merrill, Susan, 99
Metivet, Reine, 33–35
Mitchison, Naomi, 109
Monet, Andre, 154
Moody, Dwight Lyman, 178
Morgan, Lewis Henry, 130
Morrissery, Otto Andrew, 87
Mundy, Bessie, 178
Munro, Irene, 70–72
Munsterburg, Hugo, 100
Murphy, Ann, 104
Mussolini, Benito, 77–78
Myatovitch, Count, 78–79

Naylor, Mary, 93–94
Nesbit, Evelyn, 94–99
Neve, Eric, 142
Newgate Calendar, 5, 167, 171
Newman, John Henry, 15
News of the World, 5
Nodder, Frederick, 26–27

O'Donnell, Elliott, 179
Old Testament, 5
Olson, Constable, 39
Omega, Mr., 178
Ortega, Angel Rafael, 177

Palmer, Jack, 31–32

Palmer, Nelson, 32–33
Palmer, William, 166
Parkman, Francis, 176
Parkman, George, 176
Paterson, Arthur Spencer, 175
Paul, St., 91
Perceval, Spencer, 79
Petiot, 11
Philips, John, 33
Phillips, Dr., 20
Plaat, Lotte, 94–95, 156–57
Podmore case, 121–22
Pope, W. Macqueen, 80
Powell, Evan, 78, 128
Power, Patrick, 169–70
Pryke, William, 48
Pulver, Lucretia, 65–66

Radebe, Elizabeth, 167–68
Radford, Albert Bradley, 28–29
Rawlings, William, 146–50
Red Barn mystery, 47–49
Redfield family, 63–64
Redmond, William, 139
Rees, Melvin David, 161
Rhine, J. B., 152
Richet, Charles, 13
Riddell, Lord, 5
Riesenman, F. Regis, 160
Roberts, Estelle, 25–27, 109–10
Robinson, Alonzo, 11, 31, 169–71
Rochefort, Hugh, 86
Rosa, Noel, 144
Rosma, Charles B., 61, 64, 68
Rosyk (cowhand), 39, 42
Rushford, Mrs. H. H., 111–12

Samuels, Joseph, 173–74
Sandelius, Carol, 162–63
Sandelius, Walter, 162–63
Sandford, Arthur, 95
Saunders, Dr., 20
Schizophrenia, 105
Schumacher, John, 36, 37–38
Scotland Yard, 14, 15, 16, 22, 49, 51, 53, 75, 84, 149, 151–52, 171, 181

Seal, Lawrence, 83
Sequeira, Dr., 20
Shakespeare, William, 9, 128
Shaw, Commissioner, 29
Shaw, Bernard, 145
Shaw, Roland B., 16
Sickert, Walter, 12
Simmonds, Isaac, 173–74
Slaughter, Tod, 47
Smith, George Joseph, 177–78
Smith, John ("half-hanged"), 171–72
Society for Psychical Research, 56
Solomon, 5
Somerville, Edith, 72
Sonneville, Boy, 157
Speer, Harold, 74
Spencer, Frank, 143
Spilsbury, Sir Bernard, 30, 31
Spiridon, 117, 121
Stable, Justice, 175
Stead, W. T., 78
Stephens, Ian, 56–58
Stevenson, Charles, 39, 40, 42
Stories of Not Being Afraid of Ghosts, 182
Strickland, Inspector, 45–46
Sykes, Mrs., 169–70
Symonds, Yvonne Marie, 168
Szenzi family, 167

Taylor, Bill, 37
Tecumseh, 128, 129
Temple, William, 15
Tenhaeff, W. H. C., 164
Terriss, William, 79–80
Terry, Victor, 175–76
Tersinha, Maria, 144
Thaw, Harry, 95–100, 101
Tinsley, Mona, 25–27
Tombe, George Eric Gordon, 50–53
Tombe, Gordon, 50–51, 53

Tombe, Mrs. Gordon, 50–51, 53
Tonquedec, Father, 104
Tossings, Bernard van, 156
Trassjohnsky, Sara Rosa, 84
Turn of the Screw, The (James), 33

Utterson, Reg, 32

Van Dusen, C., 130
Victoria, Queen, 13
Videle, Jean, 167
Vierboom, Piet, 158

Wallace, Edgar, 181
Warren, Sir Charles, 12, 13
Webster, Professor, 176
Welborn, Curtis, 57–58
Welch, Mavis, 54–55
Wensley, Frederick, 84
West, Mae, 24–25
Whipple, Henry, 130
White, Stanford, 95–100
White raven, 6
Wickland, Carl, 97–98, 101–5
Wickland, Mrs. Carl, 97–98, 100, 104
Wilbarger, Josiah, 123–27
Wild, Jonathan, 167
Wilde, Oscar, 95
Wilkins, Irene, 75–76
Williams, Henry, 178
Williams, J. F., 79
Willis, William, 169
Wilson, Mrs. James, 110–11
Winslow, Forbes, 21
Woodhall, Edwin T., 22
Woods, Jack, 37
Wootton, Bill, 141–42
Wyllie, Curzon, 151–52

Yotopoulos, P., 115–21